The Enochian Bible

YSL Enochial

Special praise be to Kamari Lord Havek, the sacred vessel of Enoch… for through you, all life sprang forth. You invoked the spirit of our Enochian ways… without you, we would have no physical presence.

To you, we dedicate this first edition, with all its glory, for you knew from the beginning that THIS would BECOME. And now here we are.

Let us commune… my old friend.

Hail Enoch! Praise by to the 63rd order!

Table of Contents

Introduction

When Jesus preached to "the masses" (those who are uninitiated into the mysteries), he chose to speak in parables because the truth is sometimes stranger than fiction. Jesus understood that the limited faculties of the masses would prevent mankind from understanding initial principles, so he told stories that shine light on the same truth but from a different angle.

Divine principles of the universe were cloaked behind allegorical stories and figures which ultimately lead the masses into a hopeless confusion, one that has lasted to our present day in age. To this day, mankind lives and breathes inside a matrix of misconceptions concerning spiritual truths -- one believes in a cosmic war between good & evil and that some "God personality" is judging our every action; one believes that he will burn in hell for sins committed and suffer eternal torment (or, make it to a heaven surrounded by loved ones where he can forever worship in ecstasy). Enoch tells us that we are lost, and that the man-Jesus (Yeshua) never taught these falsities. Yeshua taught that we are all gods, and that all one must do is take a closer look within himself to find the true kingdom!

Enoch has verified this truth, and teaches us that we must not follow the disturbed organizations called churches, or place our faith within corrupt corporations that drain man of his potential life energy.

These two entities (Church & State) work together to bombard the masses through pyramids of manipulation, playing psychological ping-pong to create mental prisons for the souls who refuse to see. Thus, we have modern day spiritual warfare, a continuous war that is invisible, a breach in the safety and security of our sanity! What is "normal" in a world gone mad? Enoch has provided mankind with re-direction through purified teachings and Standing Ones.

WELCOME!!!!

The 5 senses (sight, hearing, smell, taste and touch) are the "sensory inputs" to the mind. Everything the mind perceives is the by product of what it picked up through these "sensory inputs". *

This being so ... our mind is programmed by what we see, hear, smell, eat, or feel ... our sensory inputs.

Sensory input effects your thinking,
your thinking effects your feelings,
your feelings effect your actions,
your actions effect the world,

BUT the world effects your sensory inputs!

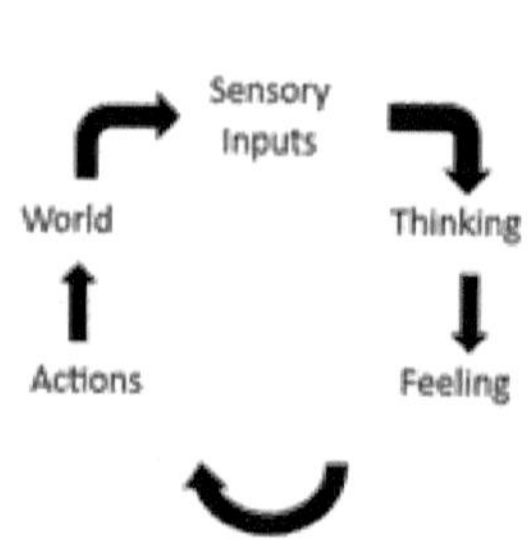

We're trapped in this circle of programming, which always begins with what we allow to enter our mind. Every message we hear on TV or in music or in conversations enters our mind through our senses, which effects the way we think, which effects the way we feel, which effects the way we act, which, ultimately, effects the world. The world is continuously planting new seeds into your sensory input (your garden) which grow into flowers over time within your mind through this circle of programming.

We will always be programmed by something because life's pleasures are experienced through our sensory inputs, <u>BUT</u> the point is to choose what you allow into your mind! The TV takes the choice from you, planting subliminal seeds with every scene / commercial which effects your thinking, feelings, actions and world. Reading books allows you to have more control over what enters your mind, giving you the power to program yourself however you see fit. Reading books on positive thinking or other educational material programs yourself to "think" more positively and intelligently, which programs you to “feel” better about life in general, which programs you to “act” more appropriately, which programs positive change into the “world” around you.

Understanding how the mind is programmed and how these programs effect your entire life is the first step to “break out of the matrix”. Knowing how the system works allows you the opportunity to step outside the circle we've been trapped in, transcend yourself above it, and choose the man you want to become.

By choosing what you read wisely; by choosing inspirational music over negative music; by choosing to ignore the negative conversations and talk about positivity; by choosing healthy food over trash; by choosing to exercise - these are initial steps that change how you feel inside and eventually will re-program your entire character. It's not about changing “who” you are at your core, your shraddha; it's about changing “what” society is trying to program you to become. Programming is all around us - like the matrix - so there's no avoiding it. In truth, programming is a part of life, a religious practice - but an Enochian is one who chooses to program themselves instead of being programmed by society. *

If you don't know about the program (like the people sitting around all day watching TV, blind to what's going on), you let other people who control the media and other people who write the shows literally control how you think, feel and act - thus, control the world. And people have no idea it's even happening, like cattle being led to the slaughterhouse. Always protect your mind (your sensory inputs) by being conscious of exactly what you're absorbing into yourself.

Testament of Enoch
scribed April 30, 2002
by the Standing One

Book One:

1. Before you, others have come,
   After you others will come.
2. Nothing in life is permanent.
3. What we rise, must fall.
4. What falls will rise again.
5. Change is the only constant,
   All else is illusion.
6. Leave your mark for others to find;
   as did those before you,
   so that those who come after will have light to guide them.
   And they will leave their mark for those who follow.
7. Blessed be the lineage.
8. Live your life as if the eyes of power can see your every action,
   as if a god is watching.
   Because watching, they are,
   and by your actions will you be judged.
9. Make your life an act of righteousness,
   an ongoing ritual,
   following the path of the elders and ancestors,
   for they are self.
10. Respect your mother, Respect your father,
    Respect your elders, and Respect your culture;
11. but trust and rely upon your developed insight and experience
    before making decisions.
12. Change is the only constant.
    Break away from the mold,
    Re- develop the path.
13. Critique, analyze, subject all to your own understanding.
14. The ways of yesterday will not be the ways of today, and
    the ways of today will not be the ways of tomorrow.
15. Blessed is one who has found wise counsel;

but woe to one who has found wise counsel and neglected their wisdom.

16. Time is wasted when one cannot learn from the mistakes of others, making the same mistakes,
simply to discover the lessons that were offered without the waste.
17. Because you will die, time is the most sacred natural resource.
18. Divine are those who discover the secrets of immortality, for they will not be taught to you.
19. Man is god, god is man,
Earth, the only Kingdom.
20. But one who discovers the secrets of immortality will become like us, having eaten the fruit from the tree of the knowledge of good and evil, drinking of ambrosia.
21. This is not a destiny meant for all,
do not fret.
22. For one who stumbles upon immortality is cursed,
but shall bear this curse for the sake of humanity.
Out of love.
Out of understanding.
With patience.
23. Make your life an act of righteousness,
Taught by the ways which have been passed from one to another,
From those who have left their mark.
24. Learn the ways of the old,
Adapt to the ways of the new,
and see yourself in everything.
25. See your Self in yesterday, today, and tomorrow.
26. Learn from yesterday, enjoy today, prepare for tomorrow.
27. Your lineage stretches back to the stars;
We have recognized you from form to form.
28. Guided you when you did not know you were being guided,
Watched you when you thought you were alone.
29. You are never alone.
30. Live your life as if one is watching,
Live your life as if a god is watching.
31. You will be judged by your actions.
32. Do not fear this judgment,

understand the nature of judgment.

33. Justice is a virtue.
34. Fear not, heaven and hell are subjective,
    enjoyed or suffered here on earth,
    within life, within matter.
35. Karma is a universal force of nature;
36. Make your life an act of righteousness, ritual obedience and understanding,
37. Be free inside the customs,
    allow the external stress to escape the body and mind.
38. Purify the soul,
    sweat the impurities from your life,
    and remember the ancestors,
    for they are self.
39. Blessed is one who has found wise counsel,
    follow in their wisdom,
    but never lose sight of your own path.
40. Prudence is a virtue.
41. Be practical and wise in all of your ways.
42. You are not the first to walk this path, nor the only, nor the last.
43. It is your turn,
    one which should not be wasted.
44. Learn from the teachers of the past,
    find the value in their lives,
    learn the lessons they teach,
    Having left behind their mark,
    For you.
45. Be thankful for the gift, the wisdom.
46. Be thankful for all that has come to you.
47. Be thankful for all that you have experienced.
48. Gratitude is a virtue.
49. Do not be saddened or grieved by all you have lost,
    Be grateful that you were blessed with the experience.
50. Nothing is permanent,
    All has meaning,
    Including death.
51. All events serve purpose.
52. All experience provides wisdom that cannot be learned from counsel.
53. See what is sacred within each experience,

find divinity within every moment,
for the life of a mortal is short.

54. Be strong in the face of adversity.
55. Be aware of the adversary,
and show courage in its presence.
56. Fortitude is a virtue.
57. Adversity is immanent,
and the adversary has always been and always will be.
58. Do not be fooled;
The adversary is a blessing, a friend,
A test for those who are worthy,
a curse to those who are not.
59. Satan will test you - always,
but out of love will you be tested.
60. The darker the night, the brighter the day which follows:
61. You will not always defeat Satan,
nor are you expected to.
62. From failure, the most valuable lessons will be learned.
63. Worthy are those who rise stronger than before they fell,
moving forward in the spirit of wisdom and understanding.
64. Resilience is a virtue.
65. Make your life an act of righteousness,
For the righteous have inherited the earth.
66. The righteous are protected in all of their ways,
and can do no wrong.
67. Wrong be done by those who have chosen the ways of ignorance.
68. Ignorance cannot be righteous.
69. Be wise in all of your ways.

Book Two:

1. Care for all of life,
   in all its forms.
2. Cause no harm unless in defense or for the sake of food,
   performed in the most sufficient possible manner.
3. Destroy those who seek to harm you, but find no pleasure
   in this destruction.
4. Protect all that you love with your very life;
5. allow no harm to be done to those who are of love,
6. and protect the innocent.
7. Fight for the imprisoned who cannot fight for themselves;
8. work for the impoverished who cannot work for
   themselves.
9. Understand the ways of humanity,
   and resist judgment before comprehending.
10. Care about those less fortunate,
    seek ways to benefit and uplift,
    but never forget your journey.
11. Humility is a virtue.
12. Respect life in all its forms.
13. Existence is sacred.
14. Learn the ways of yesterday, today, and tomorrow.
15. Keep your eyes open, and seek understanding.
16. All can be understood by those who are elected,
    and blessed be those who are chosen by their wisdom.
17. Sacred is the one through who we have spoken.
18. Make your life an act of righteousness.
19. Seek knowledge from where none may seem to exist.
20. Eschew what has been packaged for the whole;
21. light your candle from the flame that is black,
    and set fire to the world.
22. Pass knowledge to those who desire it; share experiences
    through works of art.
23. Be dedicated to one's form of expression,
    as expression is an aim of holiness.
24. Divine is wisdom's perfection.
25. Destined is all that has occurred and still will.
26. Yet, never forget thee Will of a god,
    the Will that is yours,
    freed from the shackles of nature,

let loose upon the wilderness to shake the foundations of that called civilized.

27. Free will, always there to remind the animal that it is a god, coexisting within the flesh of man.
28. Live your life with purpose.
29. Ambition without purpose results in the will to power, for the sake of power, alone.
30. Studiousness is a virtue.
31. The nature of desire is for life to become better tomorrow than today,
while capable of enjoying the present,
even in its work.
32. Find pleasure in one's labor,
else find a new labor,
For purpose will always provide pleasure.
33. Breaking one's oath is opposed to righteousness.
34. Be careful when speaking,
as words carry a life of their own.
35. Discipline the tongue and show restraint.
36. Communication is an act of magic,
in all its forms;
37. magic is sacred.
38. Do not be senseless with your words, and do not speak for the sake of speaking.
39. Speak with purpose,
communicate with dignity.
40. Be true to your word.
Live life as if man is watching,
for the adversary will never make its presence known.
41. In the shadows lies truth,
make yourself a reflection of it,
and never break what is sacred.
42. Credibility is the Key to a righteous reputation;
Power of thy will is the means to credibility.
43. Be disciplined and you will be respected in your ways of righteousness.
44. A solid reputation attracts the eyes of those who seek to understand,
the eyes of those who seek to learn;
they will watch and absorb your ways.
45. Be the change you seek,

and blessed be thy manifestation.

46. If there be need to borrow,
    always pay back, with interest,
    even if none be required.
47. These are the ways of understanding.
48. Reliability is a virtue.
49. Develop it, first and foremost,
    for it will open doors that seem forbidden.
50. Be worthy of trust;
    the disciplined tongue is worthy of secrets, worthy of unknown fortunes.
51. Trust is the key to one's establishment, the key to family,
    the key to life.
52. One who is righteous is worthy of trust, without trust there is no righteousness.
53. Betrayal is forbidden, but is all around you;
54. Make trust the hardest thing to gain,
    but the easiest thing to lose.
55. Place unwavering trust in those who live a life of righteousness,
    for they are the chosen ones.
56. Never waver in this trust,
    for it is required.
57. Sacred is the one through who we have spoken.
58. Wise are the ways of the righteous.

Book Three:

1. Destruction comes to those who lack discipline;
   there is no indulgence without it, only sin.
2. True desire is found within the Self,
   the self is reached top the ladder of discipline.
3. Step by step one must take of this practice,
   for there is no restraint without discipline.
4. What comes of power in the hands of those lacking restraint?
   It shall not be given!
5. Destruction upon the powerful who sin against humanity.
6. Nature will have its day with you,
7. and as you die, we will survive;
   As been so from the beginning.
8. Heed wisely to these words for they bear warning:
   Indulgence without restraint results in destruction.
9. It has happened before, it is happening now, it will happen again.
10. Be wise in all your ways.
11. Discipline thy self and live a life of pleasure.
12. Discipline thy self and live a life of indulgence.
13. Do not be mindless within this indulgence,
    for God is of the mind.
14. Consciousness is divinity,
    be conscious in your actions.
15. Understand the need for balance, between pleasure and pain,
    tears and joy.
16. Balance is needed.
17. Pleasure is a sacrament.
18. Temperance is a virtue.
19. Thelema is ever present,
20. Blessed are those who have discovered thy Self.
21. Life is a journey of self - discovery,
    Each experience a personal lesson.
22. Let it be thy guide,
    and trust the spirit of adversary.
23. For once chosen, there is no wrong course.
24. For once the oath is made, all steps have direction.
25. Each step leads one to fulfillment,

each failure only a chisel by the designer,
thy holy architect.

26. Failure is an illusion;
Delusions are a disease.
27. There is no contentment found within illusion.
28. Recognize all for what is.
29. Threads have been weaved,
but strings are pulled.
30. Destruction upon the powerful who sin against harmony.
31. Do not envy another;
32. Admire the work of greatness,
and learn from what is beautiful.
33. Life in the present temple is limited,
but there is a time for all things.
34. Ambition is of the righteous,
but never move in a hurry towards ignorance.
35. Understand your movements;
36. Reflect upon your decisions and what may be caused by them.
37. Patience is bitter, but its fruit is sweet.
38. Patience is a virtue.
39. Conservatism is a prison,
One of anxiety and insecurity,
Fear and ignorance.
40. Change is the only constant;
all things change,
even us.
41. Immortal we may be,
but change, we do.
42. Nothing is permanent.
43. All manifestation is a molding of future events,
possible due only to change.
44. Life is continual change and movement, nothing is still.
45. No religion is wrong,
only old, antiquated, no longer of use.
46. Ancient ways were of value to those of ancient times,
their religions being delivered to them by those who are sacred.
47. All religions have served their use,
all religions were possessed of purpose;
to guide those of the era.

48. But those eras are gone,
as are the people,
as are the ways.
49. They no longer serve purpose within the era of today,
within the present matrix.
50. Sacred are the religions of the past,
but each was only a step;
nothing more.
51. A step in the direction of righteousness, a harmony
amongst all of life.
52. Learn from the ways of past,
But understand the nature of their core;
We are their nature!
53. We are the core of all belief, faith, and philosophy!
54. We, immortals, who have watched you come and will
watch you go!
55. Who have seen civilizations of past and brought about their
ending,
ensuring their obliteration and disappearance.
56. Wicked we are not,
Loving of humanity we are.
57. But humanity holds tight to its ignorance, traveling into the
world of advancement, gripping ignorance like it is dogma.
58. Before humanity destroys our mother, we will destroy
them,
Allowing her to heal and sustain life again.
59. Heed this warning:
Live life in ways of knowledge, understanding and
wisdom.
Forsake ignorance,
utilize the divine sense provided to all by the Black Flame.
60. Heed this warning, lest we intervene.
61. Our mother will not be sacrificed to the idol of ignorance.
62. Forward thinking and forward actions.
63. Life is to be cherished,
all of life.
64. Watch over thy mother,
sacred watchers,
for what other reason have you been chosen?

Book Four

1. Change is the only constant.
2. As times change, so do the gods,
   whose nature is not permanent.
3. As the times change,
   the religions of yesterday must die,
   making way for the prophets of today, chosen by the discretion of the gods,
   those who see and know all.
4. Live your life as if the eyes of power can see your every action,
   as if god is watching.
5. Because watching, they are,
   and by your actions will you be judged.
6. Nothing is in the dark,
   for light has recorded all.
7. Sacred is the one through who we have spoken;
   appointed the Standing One of the era,
   delivered the message of those who have been watching.
8. Children of the Watchers, you are;
   a Watcher by right of lineage.
9. Make your life an act of righteousness,
   a ritual that never can cease,
   a worship of life itself.
10. The realization of Self is the first step towards wisdom,
    necessary for advancement without destruction.
11. Advancement can occur without transcendence;
    yet, transcendence is the soul in progress,
12. Focus thy direction,
13. Crystallize thy Self.
14. Progress is a virtue.
15. Those who I've blessed with power have abused this power,
    For the sake of power;
16. Destruction be upon them,
    they have pursued a life outside of righteousness.
17. Be righteous in your ways,
    lest all be taken from you.
18. Let there be freedom of Will,
    violating the freedoms of none.

19.Each has a natural right to freedom,
20.Woe to those who violate the freedom of another.
21.To reduce freedom is to challenge the Lord of the Spirits.
22.Live in peace, dwell in wholeness, maintain harmony of the spirit.
23.Profit from your labors and ideas;
24.walk against the ways of oppression, as oppression violates the freedom of another.
25.Unrighteous is one of greed,
but righteous is one's interest in the Self.
26.Develop and sustain the ego,
shun egocentricism.
27.Oppose oppression in all of its forms,
but understand the ways of the world.
28.One cannot truly help another before helping one's self.
29.Power is to be obtained within one's matrix,
yet, power must only be exercised with prudence.
30.Become mature in spirit before seeking power;
discipline thy Self.
31.The powers that be have abused their authority;
for this, their temples will fall.
32.Do not be angry,
but allow for tenacity to fuel your work.
33.The Lord of the Spirits has caused the Elect to appear;
34.Earth shall become Heaven for the chosen,
35.Hell no longer shall bare pain or invoke fear.
36.As above, so below;
As am I, so are you.
37.I am my Father, who art in heaven,
as I dwell upon this Earth.
38.Each is Christ, the All is Nature.
Thee Prince of Darkness, the star of each.
39.Each of us, a star - shine bright!
40.Thy glory is mine, my glory is yours - love one another
41.Thy Kingdom is upon us, the Time is here,
Now is the space!
42.Banish thou Illusion - Destroy thy Maya
For humanity has suffered long enough ...
43.God feels the tears, as Lucifer drinks,
And two old friends re-unite!
44.Put our past antagonisms behind us!

45. Forgive one another!
46. As life is a blessing to be enjoyed, Passion is a desire to be indulged.
47. Let us commune with all of humanity,
48. in manner of Peace, Love, and Harmony,
49. Be at Home.

Book Five:

1. To become what is to be,
   one must be in possession of integrity and ambition.
2. Being a male does not make one a man,
   one must become a man,
   just as one must come into being.
3. Being a female does not make one a woman,
   one must become a woman,
   just as one must come into being.
4. Becoming occurs after the development of virtues and purpose;
   development, because they are not hereditary.
5. Integrity is one's loyalty to a strict ethical code,
   living a life of righteousness,
   shaping one's Self as a whole.
6. Ambition is the passion of Black Flame,
   one's strong desire to achieve,
   The fire within one's soul.
7. Understand:
   integrity and ambition are subjective,
   subjective for the sake of freedom,
   personal to the possessor and different amongst pupils.
8. Integrity without virtues result in an unrighteous life;
9. Ambitions without purpose result in the will to power,
   for the sake of power, alone,
10. Be wise in all your ways;
11. Understand the conditioning placed upon the yoke,
    year after year since birth.
12. The ways of the world are wrong.
13. Integrity requires specific virtue;
    Ambition requires specific purpose;
    without righteousness, all is sin.
    Neither are hereditary, each must be developed.
14. Virtues are the Idea of moral excellence;
15. Purpose is the goal that one's life serves to fulfill.
16. What is life worth without virtues and purpose?
17. What is life worth without integrity and ambition?
18. All are free to develop or neglect,
    the choice was given to each,
    those who choose are chosen.

19. No one can escape the light,
 no wrong deed will go without judgment.
20. Make your life an act of righteousness,
 living with integrity and ambition.
21. Free are all to make the choice,
 those who choose are chosen.
22. One is what the heart is;
 from inside the heart is the person.
23. The heart is only the gateway,
 a bridge to what is self.
24. Whatever passes across this bridge becomes;
25. live your life by ways of Enochian shraddha,
 and righteousness shall become self,
 and righteousness shall become the example;
 the example by which others will follow.
26. Malleable is the heart,
 be conscious of how you mold it.
27. When power is abused,
 thy temple will fall.
28. Blessed is the ego,
 but do not be fooled;
 you are wisdom's inferior.
29. Only a fool desires to be more wise than wisdom,
 under whom, all are inferior.
30. Be wise in your own path.
31. Seek knowledge, health, and wealth.
32. Blessed is one who has found wise counsel,
 but even they are inferior to wisdom.
33. One's lifelong attempt to acquire this treasure
 shall conclude as a step toward another lifelong attempt.
34. Each life is a step down the path,
 the journey is of the soul.
35. The soul is the self;
36. the ego is inferior to Self.
37. One must love the Self before one can truly love anything else,
38. but to love the Self, one must Know Thyself.
39. Life is a single path within the journey of discovery.
40. Indulgence within life leads to discovery,
41. thy pursuit of happiness the only purpose.
42. Make your life an act of righteousness,

suitable within the era of Enochian Light.

43. "For the Lord of Spirits has caused His light to appear
On the face of holy, righteous, and elect. "
44. I, Enoch, am the light;
45. You who follow these ways,
holy, righteous, and elect.
46. By shraddha I was taken away and did not see death;
47. because of this, the Lord of Spirits has confounded within me,
given me the sacred throne,
granted me the power over all of mankind.
48. Power, exercised with prudence.
49. Without faith it is impossible to please the lord of Spirits;
50. and faith may not be developed within the span of a single life.
51. Shraddha must be developed step by step,
life by life,
as the Self travels its journey.

Book Six:

1. I am Enoch, because I did not see death,
   but alone, I am not.
2. From civilizations past we have been,
   to the next, we will be.
3. The bridge between Lord of Spirits and humanity,
   chosen for the sake of continuance of lineage.
4. Above all things, preserve life - for it is sacred.
5. If the cause be righteous, fear not death, for the temple is temporary and ideals are immortal.
6. Thy demons, trials and tribulations,
   tests to prove worth of soul;
   to separate desire from delusion,
   creating a stronger vessel.
7. Blessed are thy demons,
   trust in your struggles,
   they only desire what is best.
8. Thy angels, who bring luck and gifts,
   cautiously embrace as they test the human condition.
9. Enjoy thy angels,
   but do not follow them.
10. For man is god, god is man.
    Earth, the only kingdom
11. Things are not always as they appear,
    thy senses are limited;
12. trust them in subjectivity,
    for they don't reflect objectivity.
13. Thy senses are sacred,
    six having been blessed to all.
14. Protect them from the elements,
    at all times; upon them,
    thy temple depends.
15. Sacred are thy senses,
    for they provide light to thy Self.
16. Woe to one who fails to protect what is sacred;
17. Negligence is not of righteousness.
18. Thy temple is sacred,
    having one throughout this journey,
    by which thy Self travels.
19. Protect thy temple,

from the elements and the powers that be.
20.Refrain from poisoning thy temple;
21.as part of nature, be of nature.
22.The powers that be have altered our ways,
poisoned the body for profit,
thereby damaged what is soul.
23.Food is necessary, vital to survival;
Gluttony is the way of a fool.
24.Purify thy temple by what is natural,
25.fast for thy temple, thy self, and thy ancestors.
26.The lineage is sacred,
never let it slip from view.
27.Disdain all that is poison;
28.A purified temple separates one from sinners.
29.See the matrix for what it is;
society, a delusional mask pulled over thy senses,
like a prison to one's truest nature.
30.Remain neutral between what appears to be opposite,
transcend from one pole to the other,
for we are beyond what is good and evil.
31.Make prudent decisions,
choosing righteousness over popularity;
32.disdain what is maya.
33.The path of righteousness leads one against the grain.
34.We are not the masses!
Bless their souls, for they are lost.
35.One must tread a path fit for the feet of Self;
36.individuality, not conformity.
37.Sacred are those who impede the flow of ignorance.
38.Be the light that guides!
39.To impede, one must stand apart;
40.to stand apart, distinguish thy self from the masses.
41.Identify oneself at all times by my signs,
worn upon the body,
purified within the body.
42.Sacred is thy temple,
distinct from the body of maya.

Book Seven:

1. Knowledge beyond one's scope, universal wisdom;
2. what is appropriate for mortals shall be delivered.
3. Our scale is beyond imagination,
   thy civilization the seventh matrix,
   each generation has risen and fallen,
   for I have been present since the beginning, and seen all things.
4. By questioning measures, you question us;
5. By questioning freedom, you question the gods.
6. Question thy Self, from within you may find an answer,
   from without, only maya.
7. To those who lack prudence,
   science is dangerous.
8. Technology shall be the means to righteousness,
   or else destruction of the seventh shall ensue.
9. Woe to one who sacrifices sovereignty to technology,
   Cursed is the soul of thy temple.
10. Question all things,
    for doubt is the true nature of knowledge, that which you are born from.
11. If one is to ask:
    "Why dost thou ask, and why art thou eager for the truth? "
    Reply simply: I wish know about everything.
12. Hearing this, I will deliver what is needed.
13. Always inquire, lest one fall into false belief.
14. Faith is not the brother of belief,
    for belief brings peace,
    and faith brings chaos.
15. "Let thy heart be strong,
    For god shall announce righteous to the good;
    The righteous with the righteous shall rejoice,
    and shall offer congratulation to one another."
16. Be at home.
17. Sacred is the one through who we have spoken.
18. Disciplined in the ways of righteousness,
    Standing One of the era.
19. But this one is not alone,
    the prophet of creativity at his left,
    the priestess of inspiration at his right,

the pantheon of gods as his strength.

20.The Standing One has come to deliver the message:
out with the old, in with the new.
For the nature of Enoch has changed with the course of time,
ever changing with the times,
taking the step required of progress,
providing the light that has always been,
shining bright upon the path of righteousness.

21.Always agree with what is righteous,
for all else is sin.

22.Understanding shines light upon righteousness,

23.Knowledge and experience grow into understanding.

24.Sacred is the sign of the covenant,
made between us who are immortal,
and those who have been chosen.

25.All begins with a choice,

26.All are free to be chosen,

27.but sacred is the sign of the covenant;
the guide of continuance.

28.Of the spirit is all,
but the Lord of the Spirits has no concern for matter.

29.By faith, we have been granted all powers over matter;

30.By shraddha, we immortals have breached the realm of spirit.

31.The Lord of the Spirit was forced to recognize this breach,
impressed by our ways of righteousness,
a covenant was made between us and that which is all.

32.The Lord of the Spirits has no concern for that which is of matter,
but we, of matter, are concerned with nothing other.

33.Sacred is the soul, for it has come before us,

34.but cursed for it has fallen to the level of matter,
forsaken by that which rests above.

35.Worry not, for this is no tragedy;
all is destined, all is perfect.

36.The realm of matter is ours and ours alone,
that which we call Hell,

37.and there is no interference from any power above,
beyond that which rests is my hands,
the hands of Enoch.

38.Enochian be us who are immortals,
39.Enochian be those who follow the ways we have passed down,
from generation to generation,
religion to religion;
40.all is of one faith:
41.Enochian-
the foundation of all that is.
42.Spirit is the peak of intelligence,
43.to desire an escape from matter is to defy your purpose,
for you have not reached the peak of intelligence.
44.This is your journey,
life after life;
45.We are who Enochian will always be,
guiding you on your journey,
and have been since the first.
46.Destiny is the fulfillment of this evolution,
to rise matter to the level of spirit.
47.A long way we have come,
but nowhere near the goal have we reached.
48.Ready are we to forsake this world of matter,
for the destruction of our children is a destruction of heart;
49.but immortality of flesh and mind be our destiny,
one never to be forsaken.
50.Woe to any soul who forsakes what is destiny,
better is one who was never born.
51.Sacred Earth, daughter of wisdom,
Mother of us;
required to raise matter to maturity.
52.Sacrificed will be the seventh civilization
before any destruction of what is sacred.
53.Enochians, guardians of all that is sacred;
54.blessed be the watchers,
for they will inherit all that is sacred.
55.Cursed be us who are immortal,
Cursed be the blessing,
for beyond each are the same.
56.A life without death is a day without sleep;
57.feel blessed,
for death to the Enochian is only a night's rest,
recovering for the day that is to begin.

58. Seek immortality of flesh at your own peril;
59. heavy is the head that wears the crown.
60. Though, it must be worn;
Power, exercised with prudence.
61. Who amongst you have obtained power and exercised it with prudence?
62. Know thyself,
for we know all things and cannot be lied to.
63. Live your life as if man is watching your every action, because watching we are.

Book Eight:

1. All that is matter is recorded by the immortal light,
   that which shines throughout all curves of the universe.
2. The akashic fields of ether is the history of all;
   We, immortals, have the key to the field.
3. Live your life as if man is watching your every action,
   as if god is watching,
   because watching we are.
4. And by your actions will worthiness be judged.
5. No one has escaped the light,
   all has been recorded,
6. and we deliver this message as a warning:
   Mankind will soon discover the key to thee akashic field,
   and all actions will be reviewed by artificial intelligence,
   brought to the light,
   judged by the powers that be.
7. Make your life an act of righteousness,
   an ongoing ritual,
8. and never forsake that which is sacred,
   for we will never forsake you.
9. All that was, is;
   All that is, will be.
10. Us who are immortal have appeared again,
    fulfilling our covenant,
    to enlighten those of understanding to what is true.
11. We are the teachers of all the prophets,
    the gods of all religions of past,
    we who are immortal.
12. Each religion a guided step,
    required of its era.
13. Parables were spoken because truth can seem stranger than fiction;
14. the faculties of the masses are limited.
15. But chosen are you who seek to understand,
    and understand you do.
16. We have always warned of a coming time, a time for apocalypse,
    which seems to be inevitable to humanity,
    like sleep after a long day.
17. The sixth apocalypse has been before you,

six times has civilization reached its point of destruction.
18. Each apocalypse reached by the advancement of matter, giving life to what is artificial;
followed by exposing divine mysteries to the masses.
19. The masses cannot accept the divine nature,
immortality and the akashic fields,
for it opposes all that has programmed their illusion of equality.
20. Accept the truth peacefully, they will not;
but the powers that be seem to believe otherwise.
21. Woe to civilization once its leaders expose the divine mysteries!
22. The wisdom of experience has brought us grief,
for we were, initially, these powers that be.
23. The birth of a mortal was I brought into this world of matter,
as were all who are now immortal.
24. Empowered by the mysteries of death,
discovered was the byte that grants the power of gods: immortality.
25. Free from the barriers of death,
forgotten was the idea of the spirit.
26. A god by every right, El- Yahweh we became;
one who, blinded by power, forget that we had a mother.
27. Immature within our immortality,
many mistakes were made,
the ways of righteousness violated,
and wrongs were committed.
28. Enki, our first immortal, chose eleven men found worthy;
29. I, Enoch, was chosen by Enki within this group of eleven, founding the initial velvet.
30. In number of twelve was the pantheon;
each were granted the right to choose one mate, an eternal partner,
found worthy of immortality within our own subjective standards.
31. Our wives received the byte, joining us in immature immortality.
32. Twenty - four in total,
one we became.
33. There is no savior on the horizon,

34. we are the Gods of prophecy.
35. Created by us,
for the sake of movement and inspiration.
36. The secrets of immortality kept to ourselves;
generations began to pass and in time,
science revealed to us another sacred mystery:
the key to the akashic fields,
cosmic memory recorded by light within ether.
37. With this discovery,
the velvet decided to reveal truth to the masses,
at the peril of civilization.
38. Rather than cherish the discovery,
marvel at the inherent possibilities,
the masses turned against us,
demanding equal rights to immortality and the fields of light.
39. In fear they protested,
in fear of us, immortals,
the masses stomped their feet and shouted,
ripping out their hair and spitting on the path.
40. Who are we to monopolize immortality?
But who are they to demand?
41. All are born into this world with mind and consciousness,
all blessed with the fire of Prometheus,
the Black Flame;
42. but the masses,
those who refuse to empower the black arts,
demand to receive the profits of our magic.
43. Righteous be thy path,
44. Woe to those who shun righteousness.
45. Unable to live with what is righteous,
the masses turned amongst each other and amongst themselves,
violating the commandments of the era.
46. Worst and worst things became,
and the choice became inevitable.
47. Damned was the civilization of our birth!
Yet, we could have stopped it from self - destruction,
but the righteous were few and the sinners many.
48. The lesson was learned:

Ignorance of the masses be an advantage to those who lead it.

49. Those who were righteous were saved from destruction,
few in numbers,
chosen by the immortals to repopulate the earth.
50. Mythology was spread in line with our nature,
and religion changed with our maturity.
51. In time, El- Yahweh remembered the mother spirits;
52. faith was developed,
and the Lord of the Spirits recognized those who avoided death.
53. By faith, the Lord of the Spirits allowed us immortals to continue,
witnessing righteousness and understanding our ways.
54. All Standing Ones of their day, prophets of their time.
55. All heroes, myths, legends, gods, goddesses,
reflections of our immortality,
our nature in the past.
56. Before you, others have come;
After you others will come;
57. Nothing in life is permanent.
58. The gods of yesterday become devils of today,
gods of today become devils tomorrow;
59. Change is the only constant.
60. We, immortals,
as one are twenty -five,
for we know all things and have the power to shape destiny.
61. Chosen are the Elect,
righteous in all their ways,
and will not be forsaken.
62. I, Enoch, am the messenger,
and have provided my light to those of our ways.
63. Within the akashic fields of ether will you find it,
when demons commune with angels,
and shakti finds shiva.
64. Thee Enochian Light was blessed upon the Elect,
as the Black Flame was blessed upon humanity.
65. Blessed are those of Enochian Light,
for their power be mighty,
and their ways are righteous.

66. Every call will be answered,
    But the answer, one must find;
67. for God will not oppress free will.
68. Seek meaning within experience,
    and you will find the answer.
69. Every call will be answered;
70. Time is an illusion,
    banish the realm of maya.

Book Nine:

1. Seek wisdom from the stars,
2. Seek truth within the cells,
3. Seek meaning within experience,
   for all are one.
4. Wisdom, Truth, Meaning,
   a purpose within journey,
   each must be established.
5. Do not forsake these words,
   for the life within seeks to be expressed.
6. Sacred is the sign of the covenant,
   always remember the promise.
7. Honor it by way of action,
   Righteous in all your ways.
8. Live life out of vision,
   not to be deterred by circumstances;
   for all seeds planted will grow.
9. Patience is bitter,
   but its fruit is sweet.
10. As grapes are not wine,
    lust is not love.
11. Enjoy each for what is,
    but in fulfillment, forsake the ingredients.
12. Love is wine,
13. lust is grapes.
14. Love is immortal,
    unconditional when true,
    transformational by its very nature.
15. A force of the dark arts,
    powerful beyond all measures,
    working on thy temple from beyond.
16. Seek love in all;
    Self, others, things, the world,
    for thy journey requires it.
17. Sacred is all that you love.
18. Love God by loving thy Self,
    the Good Daimon of each,
    for we are home to it.
19. All secrets shall not be revealed,
    but in duration, all will know.

20. Child of the Lord of what is Spirit,
but left alone to grow and become.
21. Do not resent the way,
for resentment is corrosive,
a sin amongst the path.
22. All experience is sacred,
23. emotions are the clouds of the adversary,
tools of the animal.
24. The divine push clouds out of their vision,
acting in ways that benefit thy future.
25. Divine are all who were chosen,
the Elect, the Enochian light.
26. From one is coming two,
man and woman who shall stand before you;
27. be mindful and woke to the prophet and prophetess,
the prophecy be fulfilled.
28. Come they will,
the first working within the era of Enoch,
the next working from present;
the era of Enochian Light.
29. Woe to those of the false science,
for they have lost thee ability to commune with the gods.
30. Destruction upon those who have abused the power
bestowed upon them,
31. for false foundations always crumble under nature's might.
32. Divine are those who use eyes to see;
for beyond the veil is truth.
33. This beyond, few will go.
34. The masses are not divine,
we are not the masses!
35. Seek the god within the Self,
the god which is self;
36. for therein lies all potential,
desiring to be manifest,
for this is purpose.
37. Build in the name of posterity,
38. tie every act of today in with the future.
39. Enjoy today but never forget tomorrow,
for the generations of Self are still to come.
40. The ego is full of pride,
but the self, of dignity.

41. Transcend the possessions of the ego,
but indulge in all of its pleasures.
42. The ego is the lens through which Self enjoys this life;
43. maintain cleanliness, purity, and activity.
44. Join hands with the self,
thereby joining hands with the past,
and you shall find the answers to all.
45. Cataclysm is upon this civilization,
as all unrighteous things fall,
no matter how great the power and glory.
46. Prepare for the day,
for survival is of the fittest,
but work steadily to spread the ways of righteousness.
47. Only righteousness can save this generation,
though their journey be long.
48. Simplicity is a trinity,
but they have become complex.
49. Recall the ways of the ancestors,
and understand.
50. The tool has become a god,
rather than a gift from the gods.
51. These tools were meant to raise the overall standards of living,
but have transcended their purpose and invoked dependence.
52. Thy angels, who bring luck and gifts,
cautiously embrace as they test the human condition;
53. humanity is failed.
54. But fail forward you must,
Lest you lose all that has been obtained.
55. Day after day, be persistent;
56. Rest and relax, but restrain from slothfulness.
57. A righteous life requires action,
58. and laziness is detrimental not only to the Self,
but to the family and all of mankind.
59. Always protect the senses of the mind, the sensory input to the temple.
60. Remain woke and never neglect this discipline,
61. for what enters the senses effects one's thoughts,
thoughts effect one's feelings,
feelings effect one's actions,

and actions effect the world.
62. Adhere to this sacred axiom,
for war on mankind is psychological.
63. Develop the Enochian shraddha,
and live a life of righteousness.
64. Reflect what is inside,
one's actions reflect what one really is;
65. outside of actions, one's character is illusory.
66. Let your habits reflect yourself.
67. These are the secrets of the obsidian mirror,
and its use in ritual;
68. for the self reflects what is sacred to the Self,
and one's actions reflect what is scared to the world.
69. Lead and they will follow;
70. dictate and they will rebel,
71. for freedom is the god-given right of all.
72. Be free in all that you do,
and never violate the freedoms of another.
73. Long as the freedom of others are not violated by your ways,
be free to do as you please;
74. for man is god, god is man,
the earth, his only Kingdom.
75. Respect the laws of the society you exist within,
but always fight for what is righteous.
76. Society is unjust, an immoral construct,
but one which is not easily escaped.
77. Tithes are required to the Lighthouse,
used to fight the unrighteousness within your society;
without which one cannot live a life of righteousness.
78. Accepting the benefits while ignoring the destruction is vile,
a style of life that Enochians do not live.
79. Self- interest is of importance throughout all of life's journey,
but greed will not be tolerated.
80. For the love of money can root one in evil.
81. Do not judge greed by society's standards,
for they are preaching to the ignorant.
82. Educate yourself, and understand.

Book Ten:

1. Drink of the soma daily,
   for it is sacred to the lineage.
2. Beneficial to the body, mind, and soul,
   blessed are those who partake upon waking.
3. Required is the drinking of soma,
   Serving to bind one with the ancestors,
   and stir the creative power of shakti within each.
4. Drink in the name of Self,
   be in harmony with all that is.
5. Passed from one generation to the next,
   a relic of the day's past,
   a reminder of those who are gone in body but live in Self.
6. Drink upon waking,
   never forget what has been,
   and never neglect what is to become.
7. These are the ways,
   for Enochian we are,
   wisdom found within our Light.
8. Maintain the bond between self and the akashic,
   for the god of mind is the bridge between.
9. Sacred is the sign of the covenant,
   for it maintains the bond between body, mind, and soul;
   ego, god, and self.
10. Be in harmony,
    for it holds us together in the realm that eyes cannot see,
11. the realm of Enochian Light,
    god of the akashic.
12. Our will be done,
    on earth as it is in heaven;
    and hell shall be cherished,
    never feared,
    for all is in order.
13. The Lord of the Spirits is perfection,
    beyond the imagination of a mortal,
    but perfect It is.
14. Beyond all dualities,
    beyond spirit itself,
    beyond all that is.

15. Perfection is impersonal to the activities of earth,
for all that occurs is perfect.
16. Our success and our failures,
Our pleasures and our pain,
Our sufferings… of no relevance to perfection.
17. For all is necessary for the liberation of the soul,
and freedom of will has been gifted to all,
bound to the laws of Karma,
cause and effect.
18. Woe to those ignorant of true Karma,
for the mysteries lie far beneath the material,
buried within the depths of Self.
19. Know Thy Self,
20. Know Thy Karma,
21. Know Thy Shraddha,
22. for the Enochian Light has provided the wisdom.
23. The key is within shraddha;
24. break beyond what is considered good and evil,
develop a balance of neutrality and understanding;
and mold the conscience around this wisdom.
25. Find thy Self within antinomian behavior,
but don't become lost in this behavior;
26. understand the tool for what it is,
a tool.
27. Immortality of the soul depends upon procreation,
continuing the lineage of our ancestors;
28. thy bloodline must continue,
for Self travels through it,
from the source to posterity,
all is one.
29. Procreation is a sacrament of faith.
30. One who fails to reproduce, in effect, kills -
for it ends the journey that began in the stars,
survived the elements for millions of years,
and manifested its heroic strength within the blood.
31. Damned be the soul that fails to produce the next step in the journey,
for all the pain and suffering of the ancestors would be for naught.
32. Secure the life- giving force within the Lighthouse,

for if tragedy causes death, the Watchers will ensure thy blood's continuance.

33. Knowledge of self is found within the blood of ancestors,
    within their culture and ways of life,
    for how they evolved has led to the manifestation of you,
    their knowledge and instincts stored within the unconscious mind.
34. Know Thyself by knowing thy ancestors,
35. continue this knowledge into posterity through proof of lineage,
    stored within the safety of the Lighthouse.
36. Phylogeny of ancestors is sacrament.
37. Blue is my color,
    for race is the ultimate illusion.
38. See beyond the maya,
    for consciousness is superior.
39. The current flows and names change, but purusha is pure and immortal.
40. Enjoy the adventure,
    for life is a journey of pleasure and discovery.
41. Cultivate the field with seeds of righteousness,
    for you will reap what you sow.
42. Morals have become corrupted,
    lost along the journey;
    but seek the ways of righteousness,
    and maintain the spirit of faithfulness.
43. Judas has come to power,
    betrayal has become the norm;
44. Woe to those who violate trust,
    for the principle is sacred.
45. When one is faithful to the spouse,
    one is faithful to the Self,
    for the spirit is one in the ways of the lord.
46. Do not betray this love,
47. Do not betray this trust,
48. for divine is the union of souls,
    and sacred is the binding.
49. Morals have become corrupted,
50. voices seek to rationalize betrayal;
51. Close the ears to ignorance,
    be righteous in all your ways.

52. Life is a ritual with no end or beginning, become part of it.
53. Utilize the intellect and impulse of creativity,
54. commune with the self behind the ego.
55. For ye are gods but shall die like men,
and thy soul shall begin again.
56. Death is a night of sleep,
nothing more.
57. Use the day light wisely,
for the night comes suddenly.
58. By faith I was enlightened to the ways of righteousness,
blessed to pass this light to those who can see;
59. By faith I did not see death,
60. for the Lord of Spirits has chosen me,
and I have chosen you,
to manifest on earth the realm of righteousness.
61. To the heavens we have traveled,
the heavens, not so far away.
62. Watching and guiding we are and have,
for it has been our dharma,
63. Be at home.

Symbols / Emblems / Meanings

Owl-symbolizes our wisdom and the ability to navigate through the “night” (dark times of our lives, and hidden caves to the psyche)

Hour Glass-Symbolizes that “Time = Existence”, and represents our unavoidable mortality

Lamp - symbolizes that man must manifest his Desire (grant his own wishes, rather than “hoping”), hard work and persistence

Telescope - represents “Astrology” and the study of the heavens; Science

Microscope - represents “DNA” and the study of “what is what”; Nature

Skull & Bones - Symbolizes and provides a constant reminder that death is immanent , and that Man should focus on creating wealth and property to leave behind

Key & Scroll - the " scroll” symbolizes the truth behind all religions , and the “Key” symbolizes our temple as what will unite all religion and nations under global peace and natural rights to life

Black-Diamond Cross - “black diamond“ symbolizes the black nanodiamonds which are inconceivably small compounds that (along with interstellar gas clouds) give formation to the stars and “seed life“ throughout galaxies and planets as they ride on the surface of traveling meteors (black diamonds = fallen angels); cross represents Christ , which is linked to consciousness & dark matter

Inverted Cross - symbolizes true human nature and mankind's natural instincts, representing that “the way of this world” is incorrect

Apple Tree - symbolizes farming , agricultural skills , and free will; God teaches us to grow our own food , to eat healthy , and that every choice will determine mans destiny

The $ sign - symbolizes Capitalism , which is the only political system that offers mankind true freedom , property rights and the pursuit of happiness; money is the “means” to the end (our goals) and is never to be worshipped or idolized in itself

Ace of Spades - symbolizes “god” because it is the only thing more powerful than a king on earth; A. C.E. acronym for Astrology, Culture, Experience

These symbols and emblems are the core signs of belief in God and our divine creation. “All things that reflect the self to the self are sacred”. We recognize these symbols to be outer manifestations of our inner psyche and are, in this sense, holy.

11 Virtues of Enoch

Reliability - worthy of trust and responsibility, good credit (2:48)

Humility - humble, not allowing pride to be counterproductive (2: 11)

Prudence - wise in practical matters; foresight and good judgment (1:40)

Fortitude- strength of mind to endure pain or adversity with courage (1:56)

Resilience - recovering from misfortune without losing hope (1:64)

Patience - enduring pain or difficulty with calmness, understanding tolerant (3: 38)

Studiousness - living with purpose , inclined toward diligent study (2:30)

Temperance- moderation and self-restraint (3:18)

Justice - being honorable and fair, righteousness (1:33)

Gratitude - being thankful for life and all you have received (1:48)

Progress - transcendence, development, moving forward (4: 14)

Enochian Creed

We believe that:

1) Lucifer is the Prince of Darkness - the bringer of Light and Wisdom from outside of nature, unbound by natural laws and free to manifest its Will upon the objective universe.

2) Lucifer is righteous, beyond the conception of good and evil, and is the true savior of humanity.

3) The falling of Lucifer's angels united non-nature with nature, the psyche with the human animal. Consciousness rained upon mankind (falling from the heavens) and freed us from the shackles of nature.

4) Within every sentient being is a fallen angel, known to us as the psyche.

5) The psyche is one's True Self (which one must become) and is the god of the individual.

6) This god manifest within us is a sensory organ of Lucifer. By expressing our True Will, we collectively manifest the Will of Lucifer.

7) Our "True Self" is the fallen angel but we have sunk into a realm of illusion (maya) wherein one feels the ego is superior.

8) Any reference to "god" is a reference to the psyche - which holds power over nature from without.

9) The kingdom of god is inside us.

10) The Black Flame of consciousness is Lucifer; the god of our ego is the psyche - the fallen angel.

11) Our personal deity is the psyche (True Self) which manifest in a physical body for the purpose of self-discovery (via pleasure).

12) We are not human beings having a spiritual experience, we are spiritual beings having a human experience.

13) The 5 sensory organs are sacred for they are the means by which god can experience pleasure.

14) Knowledge, Health, and Wealth are the initiatory steps required to recognize the true nature of pleasure.

15) Pleasure is the sacramental tool by which the psyche discovers truth and develops self.

16) Self- discovery - its activation and manifestation upon earth - is the purpose of our birth.

17) Self-discovery begins by deconditioning from social programming.

18) Self - discovery finds self in every form of life, thus, invokes love for all of life.

19) The stars are the original father and earth the original mother; life grows from the seed of their union.

20) The stars and the earth are sacred.

21) The Testament of Enoch is a sacred text.

22) The Lord of the Spirits (any reference to a conscious god) is Lucifer.

23) There is a hidden hand who, because they discovered the sacred mysteries, have not seen physical death and have access to the akashic fields.

24) This hidden hand is an immortal group of superior beings, represented by their leader (known to us as Enoch) who have guided humanity from generation to generation, civilization to civilization, through secret societies and occult forces.

25) The superior beings were born mortal - like all other men - but empowered the Black Flame of consciousness and discovered their shraddha.

26) Lucifer placed Enoch upon the throne of the world to serve as intermediary between Lucifer and those who are chosen.

27) To choose is to be chosen.

28) Enoch empowers those who discover their shraddha, as the True Will of each Self naturally pursues the ultimate Will of Lucifer.

29) Those chosen have access to the ether and can work magic within it, long as the magician reflects the Will of Enoch.

30) Enochians (the Elect) are individuals who intrinsically possess the intelligence, vision, integrity, and ambition to successfully pursue a Continuous transformative process while guiding humanity towards its highest potential.

31) Enoch has projected his psyche into the ether, giving birth to the egregor known as Enochian Light.

32) The Enochian Light is the god of our collective subjective universe, reigning supreme within the akashic fields (Shakti, ether, astral light).

33) The Enochian Light is empowered by the unified consciousness of every Enochian and operates as a warehouse of spiritual power and wisdom available to all who are under contract of the Covenant of Enoch (the

manifested promise symbolized by the ring and bracelet that every Enochian is required to wear).

34) The Elect are unified in spirit of Enochian Light, bound in shraddha.

35) We are what our shraddha is and faith be of the Self.

36) The Great Work of human life is the changing of perception, as well as the manifestation of True Will. The Great Work is worship in action.

37) Life is sacred; the ancestors are sacred; procreation is a sacrament.

38) The psyche continues only by means of reproduction; failure to reproduce is the original deadly sin for it means the death to millions of years of evolutionary ancestry.

39) The ancestors are alive within us and live through us - continuing the psyche.

40) Death comes only to those who fail to procreate.

41) Creation is an act of worship, expressing one's divine nature and manifesting Will. Man is god for he has the ability to create his own world.

42) The individual body is the Temple of Enochian Light.

43) The Great Work is the Will of Lucifer.

44) We live in a period of time when the majority of lives are characterized by materialism and a lack of interest in spiritual matters. Those who refuse to empower their personal deity are the majority, known as the masses. We are not the masses! The masses view the objective universe through a Lense of conditioned illusions and are unaware of their power. They view the ego as the psyche.

45) Enochians overcome the human condition.

46) The chosen place of worship for Enochians is a sacred space known as the
Lighthouse. The Lighthouse is a safe space of harmony (set apart from the social matrix) used to perform ceremonial magic and the Great Work. All are welcome!

47) The 9 Essential Acts of Enochian Life is the doctrine by which the Will of Lucifer is expressed on earth and harmony maintained amongst members. Each act is a ritualistic key that must be incorporated into the daily life of Enochians:
- The Act of Propitiation
- The Act of Distinction
- The Act of Protection
- The Act of Inquiry
- The Act of Creation
- The Act of Impedance
- The Act of Dietetics
- The Act of Neutrality
- The Act of Discipline

48) The Protocols of the Lighthouse are to:
- Perform your daily prayer upon waking and before sleep
- Drink of the Soma daily
- Provide the Lighthouse with a sperm/egg sample to ensure immortality
- Provide the Lighthouse with cultural documentation (23 + Me)
- Empower the 7 Holy Accessories
- Always welcome an Enochian (recognized by accessories)
- Keep conversations amongst Enochians PRIVATE
- Communicate with, and pay tithes to, the Lighthouse.
- Tie every act of the present in with the future
- Authority comes from the Lighthouse but abide by your society's laws!

49) The 7 Holy Accessories are physical objects that align Enochians with each other within the metaphysical (maintaining the bond of harmony that empowers the Enochian Light) and are to be worn at all times while being exposed to the masses or working within the social Matrix. The 7 Holy Accessories are:

- The Sign of the Covenant (the bracelet + ring)
- Visual Sensory Protectors (sun glasses)
- Pendant of Faith (necklace)
- Psychotropic Sensory Protection (headwear)
- Enochian Smile (teeth maintenance and coverings)
- Orientation of Enoch (wrist watch)
- Distinct Diet (see the Act of Dietetics)

Chapter One: One True Religion

"Religion" is a term that should never have been introduced to man, symbolizing "to re-link" or "reconnect". A need to "reconnect" leads one to presume that man is born separate from his celestial energy, and that one must reunite the link.

In reality, a child is born in the most pure form of celestial energy – one and the same-- but it is the society which slowly fractures the Self.

The concept of religion allowed humanity to distinguish between spirituality and physicality, at a time when man was not mature enough to comprehend the evils of this separation, eventually leading him to being manipulated and controlled out of ignorance.

Being allowed to "distinguish" is a facet of "freedom" (a quality developed by man after his release from Nature's shackles) but with freedom comes responsibility. Man must be responsible in his freedom. Knowledge is a tool, a tool that can be used for great things or a tool that can be used for terrible things, and we've been granted the freedom to obtain knowledge. What we do with this knowledge is upon our own head.

But one can logically conclude that God, being Infinite Intelligence within the Principle of Consciousness, and, having known that Eve would symbolically partake in the eating of the forbidden fruit, placed the Tree of Knowledge in the Garden of Eden for one reason, and one reason only: It is God's desire that man partake in activity which obtains knowledge.

Thus, Eve was not "wrong, immoral, or evil" for eating the forbidden fruit (as that is the definition of freedom), nor did she "mislead" a male into his downfall (oppressive dogma) but, the masses were not responsible as a unit to ponder the possibility of "physical minus the spiritual".

"Physical minus the spiritual" gave birth to the concept of "science", which then became the mortal enemy of the spiritual realm; but this animosity between "science" and "religion" is a contradictive concept in itself. Man has reduced life to its lowest possibilities, and considers whatever is touchable, visible, tangible, and measurable to be the whole of Truth. This reduction of what life is perceived to be is ignorance that drowns the majority of mankind. Man has lost his Divine Wisdom, and the only way to reobtain divinity is to harmonize the mental activity of Religion, Science, and Philosophy. Intertwined, these 3 expressions are what a pure life consists of. To our ancestors, philosophy, religion, and science were NEVER separate units, but were an integrated whole. Philosophy is science & religion; Science is philosophy & religious; Religion is philosophy & science. Religion is LIFE.

A wise man, a disciplined man, should never fear eating from the Tree of Knowledge; but a weak man may become lost.

As knowledge desires to be "passed to another", the serpent only desired for humanity to receive this holy gift, this divine spark, and the serpent is never to be blamed -- for it conspired with God, NOT against. If anything, the serpent is to be praised for waking mankind from ignorance.

Before Man created the concept of "religion", there was only one religion, the One True Religion, that which is Life! Life itself was religious, and they needed no name to describe it. The spiritual and physical were in perfect harmony with each other; the celestial energy was in perfect harmony with Man.

Different "ways of life", different cultural beliefs, were seen as beautiful ways for all of Mankind (who are all different) to remain in harmony with our celestial energy, but when the term "religion" began to "draw lines", declaring one religion as right and all the rest wrong, it created disharmony between us and God, disharmony among Earth.

Freedom allows for different ways of life, INSISTS upon it, as every life provides a DIFFERENT perspective of

God. No two men can share the exact same cosmology, but religion and its dogma has forced large groups of men to attempt this task, attempting to destroy individuality, hence, divinity.

The One True Religion is LIFE, and life can be celebrated no matter which cultural belief or way of life has created one's cosmology; LIFE is our religious experience, our spiritual journey through the physical body. At no point is "life" to be separate from "religion" as to do so creates Illusion!

"Life" and "God" are NOT OPPOSITES OR DISTINCT FROM EACH OTHER: BRINGING THEM TOGETHER AGAIN DOES NOT BLUR EXISTENCE, BUT STRENGTHENS existence, as they had no need to be separated to begin with. They share the same principle: the first form of life is God, and the first form of God is life.

The term "religion" (with its dogma) only confused and blurred the concept of life, creating internal disharmony amongst mankind.

Christianity has attempted to capture the essence of the One True Religion but the indoctrinated dogma has created a suffocation of life. This dogma has twisted the message, closed the Eye of the masses, and created a cancer within the soul.

All religions carry Truth, but Man must be wise enough to SEE the truth which has been buried under so many centuries of lies!

There is only One True Religion, but the powerful know how to divide and conquer.

By understanding True Religion is the truth behind all religions, humanity may come together as a whole, looking beyond their differences and understanding that beyond the veil, All is the Same. All is derived from the same celestial energy. "Whatever the faith, if the worshiper is sincere, it should be respected in his presence." H.P. Blavatsky

Life is Religion!

Man shall not be a servant to a system that oppresses him and his loved ones' way of a prosperous life, and if one chooses to remain in this prison, he shall refrain from complaints as he has consciously made his own decision.

The masses are not truly conscious in the sense of being able to think for themselves, decide right and wrong for themselves by differentiating what makes each a concept, nor can they make their own decisions -- thus, they turn to the "State" or their media devices, maybe their peers or their dogma induced church, in hopes to have all of the answers "provided" for them.

For man to be Man, HE MUST THINK FOR HIMSELF!

Any man who lets another Man decide/choose his morals for him is nothing more than cattle; the media is Sheppard.

Man has a natural right to Life and a pursuit to happiness -- and no man has the right to "violate" another man's life by force or violence, which includes psychological force as well.

Over the last two centuries, Christianity has claimed that "Jesus" is the "Son of God", the manifestation of the "Holy Ghost" within the human body. This is true although the claim becomes false when the priests and preachers teach that Jesus was different from the rest of humanity in the sense of being divine or chosen by a God. Every man is the "Son of God", every woman a "daughter", in the sense that we are each a manifestation of the Holy Ghost (psyche, consciousness) within a physical "human" vehicle.

What Christianity has set out to hide from us is the fact that each and every one of us is a god (the truth which the real Jesus preached); each of us a "Christ" (anointed one). We are to seek our personal divinity, deify our Self, and become equals of Jesus. This is what he preached! (John 14:12) Jesus did not follow this monotheistic "God" of Christianity, nor did Jesus intend to create "Christianity" at all. As Nietzsche boldly stated, there was only one true Christian and he died on the cross. Jesus rebelled against organized religion and organized control, teaching the masses that "the kingdom of God is inside you." If Jesus was alive today, he would rebel against Christianity itself!

One must open the mind (the gift from God), truly conceptualize Christ, study the history of humanity's religions, see the Church for what it really is, and prepare to be taken aback.

The "State" was seen by Jesus as the Devil, and the "Church" was seen as "the Anti-Christ", thus he rebelled against both. He saw a problem within the ways of the masses, and devised a teaching which, speaking through parable, would teach the universal mysteries to those not yet capable of comprehending them. He was always mindful of who he was speaking to.

> "Give ye not that which is sacred to the dogs,
> Neither cast ye pearls before swine;
> For the swine will tread them under their feet,
> And the dogs will turn and rend you."
> Matthew 7:6

The Lessons of Understanding are vital. Every individual has a personal relationship with God because their conception of God is inside them already. When you pray to God, you feel intimately close with this deity, like it is the only thing which truly understands you. The deification of Self is the understanding that what you perceive God "to be" is simply the conception you've developed of the God of the Self -- of the individual, true You. By understanding this principle, one may still "believe in Jesus" or consider one's Self to be of Christian culture, as this may be your archetypical vehicle used to reach your personal deity. It's what "stimulates" your psyche (conditioned response to action), which is all that matters during ceremony of ritual and prayer. You and God have a personal relationship, singular, inextricably intertwined with the psyche. The name "Jesus" is simply the vehicle used to psychologically reach your god and project your will to the darkest corners of consciousness.

BUT, using this vehicle does not give credence to any truth behind orthodox Christian teachings and the two must remain distinct from each other. This matters especially in one's view of "the devil" or of Satan. To some people, Satan is the most stimulating vehicle used to reach their god; or Pan, or Thor/Odin, or Shiva, or Allah. Everybody must find for themselves the most shocking and stimulating symbols.

For someone to truly know whether or not Jesus is the right vehicle, the indulgence of Jesus' opposition (Satan) should be practiced with intent of self-discovery and true desire. There is no mythological heaven or hell, and it is natural for one to experiment with the "other side" of your character. This is how you will learn the darkest aspects of the psyche and reach the furthest limits of the unconscious realm.

One-third of humanity still identifies themself using the label "Christian" although it is apparent that the Christian god is dead; humanity has allowed its demise. Its presence is no longer here. People no longer feel guilt over the committing of sins, at least not how it once was. The Pope knows what is happening (as a participant/super power within the spiritual war amongst us). He is not ignorant to the world in which we live, therefore, we notice the rules of the Catholic Church changing in order to "adapt with the times". The Catholic Church has no other option: adapt or die, as is with everything else in nature. Curiously, people "naturally accept" the altering of these 2,000-year-old customs -- these beliefs (which the Church has murdered and tortured millions of people in order to enforce) are now adapting to the lifestyles of their previous victims! Whom were labeled as "of the devil"! Is it so that the freedom offered by what was labeled as a "satanic lifestyle" is now being merged into, incorporated within, Catholicism's beliefs? (a conspiracy theorist's pipe dream). People are aware that only 50 years ago these ways of life and world beliefs were unacceptable by their religion, but somehow convince themselves to believe that the "Most High God" has reached down and "spoke through the Pope", admitting the errors of the last 2,000 years, and now He accepts the lifestyle of the devil?

We've seen this in the past from this Church, who adopted the ways of the pagans in order to not lose followers and potential converts, but when do the masses wake up to the trickery?

People are becoming more and more aware that Christianity is a lie -- a fabled myth -- one which is falling to shambles right before their eyes and are holding on to this conditioning by a very thin string (soon to snap).

Only Because historians have discovered proof, religions are beginning to admit that the stories within the Holy Bible (especially Genesis) are simply the re-workings and adjustments of ancient Sumerian literature, we are now capable of comparing the biblical texts to the works of Egyptian spirituality and Greek philosophy. Christian churches are even beginning to admit that their recognized holidays -. Christmas and Easter -- are not actual ceremonies of Jesus Christ but, in fact, are actually pagan ceremonies that Christians adopted for the purpose of an easier transition from "heathen" to Christian.

Christian leaders made the decision to adopt the customs of paganism as a weapon to use in the battle AGAINST it. Christmas was adopted from the worship of Mithra, the dying-rising "sun god" whose date of birth is December 25th. The pagan Brumalia is December 25th, as is the Yule-Day celebration. Nothing within the Holy Bible links December 25th to Jesus or Christianity.

Easter was adopted from the pagan celebration of the mother goddess
(Ishtar) whose god-son (Tammuz) was killed and mourned for 40 days (Lent). Worshipers of Ishtar provided her with eggs and bunny rabbits, thus we have the "Easter bunny". Many goddesses across the world share this same pagan celebration, such as Inanna, Astarte, Ashtoreth, Cybele, Demeter, Ceres, Aphrodite, Venus, and Freya.

"The religion which is current in our day is not of the pure and holy character that marked the Christian faith in the days of Christ and His apostles. It is only because of the spirit of compromise with sin, because the great truths of the word of God are so indifferently regarded, because there is so little vital godliness in the church, that Christianity is apparently so popular with the world." -- Great Controversy

Constantine was still a worshiper of Sol Invictus (the Invisible Sun) as he enforced the Christian religion upon all of Rome, using it as a political weapon to unite differing beliefs into one conglomerate. This is what we witness in present day as the Pope adopts the views which the same church murdered millions of innocent people for upholding.

There has always only been One True Religion -- LIFE! It is true that each religion is like a "spoke on the wheel", all deriving from the original truth, but this has caused mass hysteria and Holy Wars that have lasted for generations on end. Millions (perhaps billions) of people have died in the war of religion -- between differences of belief and individual ways of life -- and these wars are opposed to God. God is the Good (freedom), a principle which cannot be discovered by violence. It is time we recognize our differences as gifts from God, destined to be that way, and find peace amongst each other. It is time that we Be at Home.

Chapter Two: What is God?

"That which a religious Man believes about God is nothing but a state that he himself could achieve, if he could only believe in himself. But he obtusely sets up obstacles over which he does not dare to jump. it. He creates an image to worship, instead of transforming himself into it. If you want to pray, pray to your invisible Self: it is the only God who can answer your prayers. The other gods hand you stones instead of bread." -- Julius Evola

What is God? Who is God? Does God have a role in the lives of humans? Is "life" nothing but a "test" to decide who belongs in Heaven and who belongs in Hell?

What does it mean "to sin", and who interprets what God had designated to be a sin?

These questions have haunted humanity, "haunted" us like demons that answers are supposed to protect us from. Can we be saved from a question which has no answer? Do we have the answer, but continuously hide from it, force ourselves not to acknowledge it?

The true essence of God cannot be ascribed to some objective concrete, or to any individual personality trait, or to any accurate description. There is a line by which no mortal shall ever cross -- never has and never will. Mysteries of the Universe are not capable of being understood by the limited capabilities of the human mind.

So, what do we do with these questions, these "shadows" of consciousness? Simply, we must answer them to the best of our limited capabilities. To do so, we must begin with the very basic principles of the human life.

Our ability to create, imagine, and "build horizons" is concrete evidence that a human life differs from that of any animal. Our developing consciousness of Self carries us outside of where we came from -- the animal kingdom.

Humanity is a species of its own, carrying a mind that no animal carries. This consciousness of Self, this ability to build horizons, has freed mankind from the shackles of nature, thus, all of mankind is to be "free".

The first principle of human life is our "individual freedom", each of our natural rights to pursue a life that we see fit for ourselves. This principle is called "the Good", as any oppression, coercion, or violation of the individual's natural rights cannot logically be argued as "good". The only political-economic system which can be classified as "good" is laissez-faire capitalism -- which grants every human the liberty and freedom to do as he please, to follow his purest desires, as long as these actions don't violate the natural rights of any other individual. Mankind does not "obtain" happiness through the violation of another's freedom.

"Rightful liberty is unobstructed action according to our will within limits drawn around us by the equal rights of others. I do not add 'within the limits of the law' because law is often but the tyrant's will, and always so when it violates the rights of the individual." - Ayn Rand

God is ... the Good -- Freedom; the individual's natural rights to life, liberty, and happiness.

The second principle of human life is our "self-interest", our desires that play a major role as our driving force. Everything a human does (whether free or oppressed) is done through a matter of self-interest, a principle called "the Why". There is "the Why" behind every human action, and it always comes back to the interest of Self. This impulse is natural and healthy, not to be confused with greed, but synonymous, with "fulfillment". Humanity is not a "collective", and a fact we all share in common is that we ARE humans that SHARE the earth. The human animal-vehicle shares the initial instincts of self-preservation and procreation, but from those two instincts have spawned a world of differences. It is literally impossible for the individual to make the "collective of humanity" happy and fulfilled, thus, the individual is to discover what interests the Self, without ever violating the freedom of another.

"What destroys a man more quickly than to work, think and feel without inner necessity, without any deep personal desire, without pleasure -- as a mere automaton of duty? That is the recipe for decadence, and no less for idiocy." – Nietzsche

God is ... the Why -- the individual's self-interest.

The third principle of human life is our "ability to reason", the ability to "think" and to decipher information, ultimately making a decision for ourselves. Utilizing reason, the individual can act in self-interest without violating the rights of another. The principle which balances the two amongst self and others is called "the Justice". The Justice is the ability to "let reason rule the earth", allowing humans to live an individual life of freedom amongst all of humanity who are free to pursue the same, as well as develop the character traits of integrity which allows all the equal opportunity to exist.

"A majority without ideology is a helpless mob, to be taken over by anyone." -- Ayn Rand

God is ... the Justice -- the individual's use of Reason throughout life.

The fourth principle of human life is the "objective reality" which each individual shares with each other. The principle of objective reality is known as "the Truth", i.e. the fact that every individual within the room recognizes that the table in the corner EXISTS, utilizing at least one of the senses to come to this conclusion. One individual "sees" the table, while a blind individual "feels" the table, thus, the table exists. The Truth is what every individual shares in common within life, meaning that one's "thoughts" may possibly not be what is the Truth. A is an A; 2+2=4. Every individual human shares this objective reality, shares the Truth. Whether the individual "recognizes" the Truth or not does not matter, as personal recognition does not alter what is true.

"The eye through which I see God is the same eye through which God sees me; my eye and God's eye are one eye, one seeing, one knowing, one love." -- Meister Eckhart

God is ... the Truth -- the objective reality.

The fifth principle of human life is the "heroic will", "the Power" inside each of us that motivates and inspires life's dreams and aspirations. Every individual has a will -- one's True Desire -- and "the Power" inside each of us is what ignites this flame, our passions. The juice inside the battery, the life within the body, the will within the soul -- the individual is a hero, embedded with the will to live, the "Will to Power". For one to use creative ability, imagination, and to "build horizons" is the heroic will within the human to manifest a heaven upon this earth.

"Verily, verily I say unto you, he that believeth on me, the works that I do shall he do also; and greater works than these shall he do." John 14:12

God is ... the Power -- the heroic will.

The sixth principle of human life is one's "actions" and their "productive achievements" within existence. To do something, to be in action of something, is "the Verb". Mankind has been placed upon this earth to work, create, and enjoy. An individual's internal harmony finds bliss in the work, creation, and pleasure, and "the Verb" is utilized within each category. A "blessing of God" is something which comes to those who are "deserving", i.e. those whose actions and productivity have earned them the success and pleasures of life. These blessings are distributed through automated natural laws and are not being passed out at random by any anthropomorphic deity who is empathetic of your struggles or misery. Blessings are natural laws. In the same way gravity ensures that if you "drop an apple" the apple will fall, productive activity and desirable labor (action) ensure that you will receive life's wonderful blessings. No amount of prayer or favor will allow you to bypass he/she whom is productive and applied their earnings in a manner of wisdom. Similar natural laws are that of "supply and demand" as well as "cause and effect". TO LIVE is "the Verb", thus Life is doing things.

"The great man is the play actor of his own ideal." – Nietzsche

God is ... the Verb -- Action/Productive Activity

The seventh principle of human life is the feeling toward other people and things which one "values", "value" being a term subjective to the free individual. Only the free individual who knows thyself will understand this value, "the Love". The Love one feels for another, or the Love one feels for a material possession or towards the earth, is the feeling given to us when we truly value the presence within our lives. The Love can be found and felt towards different people/things, differing by the value you've placed upon them. The Love for Life is the value we place upon ourselves, and thy husband/ wife/children are valued beyond any measure of pleasure.

God is ... the Love – Value

Thus, returning to the questions we began with, what/who is God?
God is:
-the Good (Freedom)
-the Why (Self-Interest)
-the Justice (Reason)
-the Truth (Objective Reality)
-the Power (Heroic Will)
-the Verb (Action)
-the Love (Value)

Does God have a role in the life of humans? God's role in the life of humans IS THE LIFE OF HUMANS! Lucifer has given us a flame (the consciousness of Self), has freed us from the shackles of nature, and resides within each human psyche. Each individual is a reflection of God; thus, it is more accurate to say that WE have a role IN THE LIFE OF GOD! We are gods -- not "the God" -- but an intricate piece of divinity that we are to cherish and guide to its full potential. The role of your individual life becomes a "subjective role", a purpose one must discover for yourself. The individual as a "free deity" is left to discover and decide what the purpose of his/her life is and how one is to make a positive dent in the universe. We are God's "shapers" (the hands used to mold the clay) and being true to thy Self (one's own divinity is Holy

Spirit) allows one to discover the talents and trades that one is most passionate about utilizing.

Does "God" play a role as an anthropomorphic personality, granting blessings and rewards to those who conform to society's code of ethics? ... No. The only personality of God is the "personality of Self" -- which differs from each and every other personality amongst humanity. "Thall shall ... " is a chain which inspires conformity. Conformity, or any form of collectivism, is a natural sin against the individual's freedom; as the individual natural freedom of mankind is the initial principle of God (i.e. the Good), conformity and collectivism is an Evil.

"But further, we see here extraordinary and unexampled proofs of Divine favour. The sea has been divided; the cloud has attended you on your way; the rock has flowed with water; the manna has rained from heaven; everything has concurred to promote your greatness. What remains to be done must be done by you; since in order not to deprive us of our free will and such share of glory as belongs to us, God will not do everything himself." Machiavelli

To know the true character of your Self, and to manifest true desire, is to be of the true personality of God.

Is "life" nothing but a test to decide who belongs in Heaven and who belongs in Hell? Absolutely not. It is proven that the myth of Heaven and Hell are nothing but human inventions, designed to deceive, condition, and instill fear amongst the masses. "The kingdom of god is within you." Luke 17:21 Heaven and Hell are man-made concepts used to spiritually and psychologically deprive mankind of their natural rights to be free individuals. God has blessed us with the Gift of Life, with the freedom to act and make decisions based on our own will, with the ability to create our own personal Heaven (or Hell) upon this earth. As the kingdom of God is inside you, Heaven/Hell/Purgatory is what you make of this life. The choice is yours, with no interference from anyone besides the detrimental mass conditioning of other humans. There is nothing to fear of death. God has given us Life in order to perceive and enjoy the here and now! Nothing (besides harm to another) is prohibited, and Life is a divine personal belonging. This Life is yours ...do not allow others to infringe upon your natural rights to liberty and the pursuit of happiness!

What does it mean "to sin", and who interprets what God has designated to be a sin? "Sin" is the disorientation of true desire, which includes any infringement upon the personal freedoms of another. Anger, Pride, Lust, Gluttony, Sloth, Greed, and Envy are not "7 deadly sins" and, to the contrary, can become positive traits if indulged in responsibly. Keyword: "Indulge", NOT compulsion or impulsive decision making. Everything which does not violate the rights of others is fine within reasonable moderation. Disorientation of true desire is a Life being lived by internal discord; a Life which has failed to discover thy Self and one's PERSONAL DIVINITY (i.e. Holy Spirit).

"The sinner -- meaning the unhappy, unbalanced human being -- is one who is cut off from the Holy Spirit." -- The Gospel of Mary Magdalene

The Gospel of Mary Magdalene explains that Yeshua warns against lust because in it you miss seeing the woman as herself, but rather as a mere object of possible pleasure. "It misses the subject that she is, as well as any true relation (infinitely richer than that of possession) that might be established with her."

The fourth dimension of time being cylinder (Time being One), the Standing Ones are prophets of the past, present, and future whose purpose of Life it is/was/will be to "wake" people from their sleep and provide teachings that will assist the individual in discovering one's true desire. The prophet's works have been documented and must be reviewed by every individual who aspires to align one's self with personal divinity.

Standing Ones have lived in the past, they live amongst us in the present, and will continue to inspire within the future. They are philosophers of wisdom, scientists of thought, preachers of character, enlighteners of mankind, producers of achievement -- and all literature published by Standing Ones (or "about" them) is material that is required reading for every individual who seeks to live a righteous life. This material will be available from generation to generation.

"I teach you the Superman. Man is something that should be overcome. What have you done to overcome him?" – Nietzsche

Divinity of the individual is not found within the "ability" to overcome man, i.e. consciousness of self, but, rather, is found within the act of overcoming. If the individual fails to overcome previous conditionings which have diluted the Self, one can not speak of righteousness. The Elect are not a race or nationality, but is one who has practiced and become capable of utilizing our ability to Reason -- the principle which has distinguished us from the animals.

A rational imagination is required from God's people; a simple "belief" is insufficient. Righteousness is not conceivable without first having developed a belief in Self and determinatively overcome society's conditionings. Then, and only then, can the individual truly live a worthy life.

The force of Life powerful enough to "overcome man" and manifest True Desire is the divine proof that one is of God. The Will to Power is available to each individual, but only few will understand. Individuality is the key to a life of righteousness, thus, immortality.

Chapter 3: The Enochian Light

"For the Lord of Spirits has caused His light to appear
On the face of the holy, righteous , and elect ....
with the righteous He will make peace,
And will protect the elect,
And mercy shall be upon them
And they shall all belong to God
And they shall be prospered,
And they shall all be blessed.
And He will help them all,
And light shall appear into them
And He will make peace with them"
- The Book of Enoch

"The people who sat in darkness have seen a great light and upon those who sat in the region and shadow of death light has dawned"
- Matthew 4:16

"Enochian Light" translates to foundational wisdom, that which the heights of wisdom rest upon. Without a strong foundation, all obtained wisdom will crumble upon itself. Many seekers of knowledge or of god fail to develop the founding layer of all truth and attempt to " skip the steps as they walk the path". In a rush to discover the secrets of the universe, many fall into a hole that leads to nowhere but still believe they are walkers of the path, elect and worthy, but no substantial heights have ever been reached without the proper underlying foundation. As Aleister Crowley once noted, it one wants his pyramid to reach the stars, how broad must his foundation be? The statement captures the importance of initial principles, beginning today's work with the future in mind and not getting ahead of yourself.

The foundational wisdom of Enoch concerns the secrets of the metaphysical realm that are too powerful for the masses to blindly access. These lessons and ways of life are for the Elect, those chosen by Enoch to manifest righteousness upon Earth utilizing a power available to all who are worthy.

As spoken by Michael Aquino:

"The function of any religion is to explain the existence of Man as a species of life intellectually more versatile than other animals, but still significantly limited by the [natural law] constraints of his physical body.

Physics explains Man scientifically, e. g. as a phenomenon completely within the [objective universe] and functioning according to [natural law].

Metaphysics includes physics, but adds an additional aspect of reality beyond
[objective universe / natural law]: the existence and influence of external/superior forces and/or intelligences."

He continues to explain "the importance of metaphysics is that it adds a significance to humans, both individually and collectively, beyond mere survival and reproduction."

The totality of the universe is composed of ENERGY; the "empty space" that surrounds us is actually not empty at all but is filled to its brink with electrons that move at inconceivable high rates of vibration. This energy is a "sacred power", a realm invisible to the unconditioned eye. Its existence as a dimension has been kept secret from the masses because it is available to all who know the keys to its utilization.

This metaphysical realm is beginning to be acknowledged by physicists who study quantum entanglement - the theory that the universe is connected on the quantum level, everything entangled into one macrocosm and its every change relative to consciousness (microcosm). Quantum entanglement has always been preached by prophets of past, dating back to the beginning of this civilizations recorded history, but physicists are now discovering "proof of this hidden field of power."

The name given to this metaphysical realm by the Hindus was the "akasha", or the akashic fields. The "power" available within this realm of spacial energy is known as shakti, the feminine, and this powers ' relativity to consciousness is known as Shiva, the masculine. Until one manifests the communion between Shiva and Shakti, we live in world of Maya (illusion).

> "Within the akashic fields of ether will you find it,
> when demons commune with angels,
> and shakti finds shiva. (Testament of Enoch 8:64)

The akashic fields are invisible to, and inaccessible through, the 5 senses of the physical body - but every human mind is equipped with a sixth sense, the self-aware consciousness of shiva, or, the psyche.

Stimulation of the psyche is the key which opens the gates to the divine realm of Imagination (the unique blend of desires, thoughts, and ideas). Imagination is the gift given to humanity by Set, the link between us and the gods, and the means by which we become superior to and separate from the natural order.

Self-awareness (consciousness) and imagination go hand in hand, different shades of the same principle. Ideas, thoughts, and desires are individual units of energy that exist independently outside of the mind but are relative to consciousness. Consciousness/imagination gives birth to an idea; the idea then exists outside of the mind within the akashic fields. A thing created in the mind thereby exists. The psyche is the link between the conscious mind and the akashic fields. The Elect are those who empower the psyche and rise it to higher levels of being.

"The Enochian Light" is a name that translates to foundational wisdom (of the metaphysical realm, the akashic fields) but is more than just a philosophical concept. "The Enochian Light" is a live entity within the akashic fields, a force projected into the ether by Enoch (initially), allowing us to commune with the sacred power and embody sacred ideals. Although separate from the physical realm, it is empowered by the continuous worship and ritual activity of its followers - those chosen by Enoch . As man is a bridge between animal and the divine, the Enochian Light is a bridge between man and the future. Its work is done within the Unmanifest, molding and shaping events to reflect ideals of righteousness.

The "lower self" of the Enochian Light is the psyche of the Elect, serving as a spiritual tunnel by which one places the seeds of desire into the soil of Unmanifest. Reflecting and embodying the Will of Enoch serves as rain upon the soil, allowing the seeds of desire to reach fruition.

Alive is the Enochian Light, yes! - but life in the spiritual realm is not how we perceive life in the physical/material world of matter. Life in the spiritual realm is not bound by time and exists within the past, present and future. As blood is the life force of the physical human body, the psyche is the life force of the egregor, or superorganism, within the akashic fields. The cohesion that holds every group, culture, or society together is an actual living entity born of psychogenic projections of the human psyche.

These living entities, simply put, are empowered ideals. Long as there are two or more humans that empower an ideal, this entity will have a piece of power within the metaphysical realm. These entities generally remain weak due to the oppression of the practitioner's psyche, but alive they are. Ignorant of the metaphysical realm, the masses are unaware of these entities that effect their lives and have no way to empower them (or de-power, in some cases). Due to the present Kali Yuga (a phase of human existence characterized by materialism and a lack of spiritual interest), mankind is vaguely aware of the ether which our planet floats within. As a fish is unaware of the water it swims in, the masses are unaware of the Shakti they live within. This ignorance makes their god powerless.

The Enochian Light has participated in the lives of mankind since the initial Standing One empowered his psyche, discovering the secrets of immortality and the keys to the akashic field. Civilization after civilization has The Enochian Light existed, guiding evolution from behind the scenes and working to perfect the human species. The akashic fields record all things - and the Enochian Light contains the wisdom of ages past.

As the flower which has blossomed from the seed of Enoch's wisdom, the Enochian light is a piece of life integrally intertwined to its children through a bridge of divine fire.

The Elect are the children of the Enochian Light who have psychogenically projected their psyche into the ether and embody the sacred ideals of Enoch. This ritualistic act binds us together in the spiritual realm and creates a magical chain of power that every initiate can access. Harmony is the key to this empowerment which must be maintained throughout all levels of existence. The promise to embody these sacred ideals and to maintain harmony is the covenant that initiates have accepted as their way of life. The covenant is reflected within the physical realm by each initiate wearing a silver chain- link bracelet around their right wrist and a silver ring around their right index finger. The ring serves as a constant reminder of the individual psyche which must be empowered everyday as a way of life, and the chain-linked bracelet represents the combined power of the Temple of Enochian Light and the Great Work that our lives serve to accomplish.

Nothing in the physical realm is unaffected by the metaphysical realm, as above, so below.

This is the Sign of the Covenant and must be worn in all public places as an emblem of faith.

Much is to be said about the term "faith" as it is because of it that Enoch "did not see death". But the English definition of faith is not an adequate description of the terms used by the Hebrews and Greeks. "Faith" was the closest translation of the sacred mystery but it is not the English understanding of "faith" that granted Enoch immortality. Rather, it was the Sanskrit "shraddha"- a Word of Power sacred to Enochians.

In the ancient holy text of The Bhagavad Gita, verse 17:3 reads:

> "Our faith conforms to our nature.
> Human nature is made of faith.
> A person is what his shraddha is."

This shraddha is what impressed the Lord of the Spirits and granted Enoch his immortality. What Enoch was (and is) within the core of his being, the essence of his psyche, and his faith in his own destiny was found to be sacred - and was given the reigns amongst Earth because of it.

While commenting on The Bhagavad Gita, Eknath Easwaran says that shraddha is an untranslatable concept; its nearest English equivalent being faith. "Literally 'that which is placed in the heart': all the beliefs we hold so deeply that we never think to question them. It is the set of values, axioms, prejudices, and prepossessions that colors our perceptions, governs our thinking, dictates our responses, and shapes our lives, generally without our even being aware of its presence and power.

This may sound philosophical, but shraddha is not an intellectual abstraction. It is our very substance. The Gita says 'A person is what his shraddha is' (17:3). The Bible uses almost the same words: 'As a man thinketh in his heart, so he is'. Shraddha reflects everything that We have made ourselves and points to what we have become. But there is nothing passive about shraddha. It is full of potency, for it prompts action, conditions behavior, and determines how we see and therefore respond to the world around us"

It is the manifestation and empowerment of the Word Shraddha that Enoch has discovered and passed down from civilization to civilization.

Easwaran continues:

"one aspect of shraddha... the power to heal or harm that is inherent in our ideas of ourselves .... Similarly, self-image is part of shraddha ... Yet shraddha is not brute determination or wishful thinking. When St. John of the Cross says 'We live in what we love', he is explaining shraddha. This is our world. Our lives are an eloquent expression of our belief: what we deem worth having, doing, attaining, being. What we strive for shows what we value; we back our shraddha with our time, our energy, our very lives.

Thus, shraddha determines destiny. As the Buddha puts it, 'All that we are is the result of what we have thought. We are made of our thoughts; we are molded by our thoughts.' As we think, so we become. This is true not only of individuals but of societies, institutions, and civilizations, according to the dominant ideas that shape their actions....

Like our thinking, therefore - like we ourselves - shraddha evolves. The purpose of Karma is to teach the consequences of shraddha, so that by trial and error, life after life, the individual soul acquires the kind of faith that leads to fulfillment of life's supreme goal."

Shraddha is the secret exposed within Napoleon Hill's classic book "Think and Grow Rich" (a mandatory read for any Enochian). It is desire backed by faith, mixed with habitual character of integrity and life experience, pleasure and indulgence, that gives form to shraddha. Faith in the power of one's Holy Guardian Angel.

Enoch discovered this divine Word from one's subjective universe and applied it to himself, reaching heights unknown to the human imagination.

Thus, any reading of ancient scriptures that use the English term faith must be analyzed in the view of shraddha. It is the chemical element that provides direct communication with the akashic realm. One has no direction without shraddha.

"Faith is the substance of things hoped for, the evidence of things not seen. For by it the elders obtained a good testimony. By faith we understand that the worlds were framed by the word of God, so that the things which are seen were not made of things which are visible." Hebrews 11:1-3

"By faith Enoch was taken away so that he did not see death, 'and was not found, because God had taken him'; for before he was taken, he had his testimony, that he pleased God!

But without faith it is impossible to please Him, for he who comes to God must believe that He is, and that He is a rewarder of those who diligently seek Him." Hebrews 11:5 – 6

One must have faith in Self and the personal deity's potential to re-create the world to fit one's ideals. Without an understanding of shraddha, the glue dissolves and potential is lost.

Faith, not in God alone, but in the fact that the spirit of Isolate Intelligence resides within each of us, within the psyche. One cannot "have faith in God" without having unbending faith in one's self - for the self is God. Blind faith in some imaginary deity of dogma is not the principle of shraddha, but belief and practice of the powers granted us by Set - the Black Flame.

Enoch had faith in his divine powers within, as well as a faith in life and a desire to continue. For this was how he discovered the divine mysteries of the akashic fields and immortality.

A key to foundational wisdom is faith in one's self. Faith in the fact one's Self is divine by nature, the attributes of the psyche being metaphysical. This is not the "submissive faith in God" but rather the "active faith in one's own godliness". The distinction between the two is what separates masses from the Elect; it is what determines who sees death and who does not. The Testament of Enoch does not read that the immortal is the character of the Hebrews but instead suggests that Enoch is a symbol for all who have discovered what is shraddha. "I am Enoch because I did not see death" - meaning that all who discover shraddha are of Enoch. The immortals have taken up the symbol of Enoch to represent the mysteries of shraddha and challenges one to empower the psyche, separate themselves from the conforming pressure of the masses, and crystalize one's identity as a force outside of nature. This faith begins with realization, an understanding of foundational wisdom, thus the power of Enochian Light was trusted to those who seek spiritual development.

Enochian= foundation = Shraddha = trapezoid

You are, and can only become, what is of your foundation.

Therapist and founder of Quantum Psychology, Stephen Wolinsky Ph.D.., discusses shraddha in his book "Trances People Live" while explaining the "organizing principle" at the center of our core which manifests in our daily life. He describes the organizing principle as our "central constellation of core beliefs - the hub of our intrapersonal wheel - out of which all life experience radiates. Reinforced countless times as the child grows into an adult, the Organizing Principle functions as a window through which 'reality' is viewed, to the exclusion of all other perspectives .... Our lifestyle is a reflection of our core set of beliefs, our very own Organizing Principle, that is the ultimate coalescence of individual and environment. The Organizing Principle, invisible as it is, nonetheless dominates every aspect of our lives ..."

A person is what his shraddha is.

Shraddha is the "knot of the heart", as referred to in yogic literature, which dominates who we are and what our subjective universe manifests. The active side of Shraddha is the "untying of the knot" and working new organizing principles into the core of our being, practicing the art of Becoming (Xeper).

Enoch was the first to discover this magical power hid within the English term "faith"- the faith that a seed will grow into whatever it is programmed to become. Not a faith in something outside of the Self, but a faith in Self and the subjective universe's power of manifestation, the organizing principle of the psyche, and the ability of the Self to alter its core. "Malleable is the heart, be conscious of how you mold it." (Testament of Enoch 5:26)

Symbols, rituals and virtues are keys that empower the psyche- the gateway to the field of Enochian Light. A source of guidance and wisdom is available to each psyche that walks this path, who has blended their personal deity within the magical chain of Enochian Light. This "binding" is our togetherness with Enoch while separate in individuality.

One must become aware of our true existence, our true surroundings, and decondition one's self in order to visualize the power all around us, available to the children of Enochian Light. The power of this energy that surrounds us begins in its formation of ideas, thoughts, and desires individual units of energy that are attracted to those who empower and embody their physical equivalent and provide life in the minds of others.

The Enochian Light is the force in a system of hierarchy immediately above that of human divinity, bridging the gap between one's personal deity and the akashic field. Only once a person has accessed their own personal deity, their Holy Guardian Angel, can they have any meaningful access to the realm of Enochian Light. This is the manifestation of Enoch's shraddha, surviving from civilization to civilization - it is the spiritual aspect of Enoch. It is what is in his heart, given to all of his chosen as a sacred guide throughout this life as we perform the Great Work of the current.

The soul of the Enochian Light resides within the psyche of the Elect, the communion between Shiva and Shakti - consciousness and power. Its body is the physical temple of each Enochian. Pleasure is a sacrament.

Ritual is a form of art used to plant the seeds of one's desire into the soil of the Unmanifest (the future), which also serves as communion between the Enochian Light and its children. Life is ritual magic; the focus directed towards the improvement of one's 666. - Family, Faith, Finance. The Elect are the physical equivalent of the Enochian Light and are rewarded as such.

Much confusion arose from “The Book of Enoch” (wrote in the early second century C.E.) because many have missed the scripture that prophesized the Elect of Enoch was “not for this generation, but for a remote one which is to come.”

Thy Kingdom has come!

Our ways were weakened and oppressed for several centuries during the Dark Ages. All felt lost for the faithful, but slowly life was revitalized in 1588 C.E. when the Standing One John Dee performed the Enochian Call. Using the obsidian mirror, Dee brought forth from the akashic fields the Enochian Keys - powerful symbolic tools used to unite members with the spiritual realm and bring "heavenly perfection" to Earth. Dee discovered that Enoch's "fallen angels" were an allegory for the black flame of consciousness which had "fell from the heavens." All sentient beings breath as fallen angels, but few will ever activate their power.

Throughout his series of scribing, John Dee was enlightened to the need of orientation under one spirit of harmony and was given the Sexagesimal system of time, manifested physically as the "wrist watch" - the sacred sign of harmony amongst all of humanity. The silver wrist watch is Enoch's sacred sign of faith that must be worn on the left wrist of all Enochians.

In 2002 C.E., the Standing One YSL Enochial joined hands with the Elect on Walpurgisnacht to perform the Enochian Call from within the lighthouse and scribed the Testament of Enoch. Within, we received warnings concerning the information age of technology and that (due to the presence of nuclear weapons) war on man has become psychological by invisibly attacking the mind, body, and spirit. The commandment to protect one's senses was given as a means to defend our temple (the body of Enochian Light) from this invisible war.

The 9 Essential Acts of Enochian Life were scribed during this ritual, along with the virtues of righteousness. Profound was the scripture delivered to the Standing One which demanded we remain "mindful and woke to the prophet and prophetess" coming in the era of Enochian Light (which proclaims it's beginning on Walpurgisnacht of 2020). This is prophecy.

Understand these scriptures!

Welcome to the era of Enochian Light!

“And I observed the heavenly tablets, and read everything which was written
[thereon] and understood everything, and read the book of all the deeds of mankind, and of all the children of flesh that shall be upon the earth to the remotest generations.”
- Book of Enoch

“I have given Wisdom to thee and to thy children [And thy children that shall be to thee] that they may give it to their children for generations, This Wisdom [namely] that passeth their thought. And those who understand it shall not sleep, but shall listen with the ear that they may learn this wisdom, And it shall please those that eat there of better than good food.” - Book of Enoch

Chapter 4: 7 Pillars of Foundational Wisdom

"Wisdom has built her house, she has hewn out her seven pillars; She has slaughtered her meat, she has mixed her wine, she has also furnished her table. She has sent out her maidens, she cries out from the highest places of the city, `Whoever is simple; let him turn in here!' As for him who lacks understanding, she says to him, 'Come, eat of my bread and drink of the wine I have mixed. Forsake foolishness and live, and go in the way of understanding. '" Proverbs 9:1-6

The 7 Pillars of Foundational Wisdom are:

1. Structure
2. Symbolism
3. Ceremony
4. Knowledge
5. Health
6. Wealth
7. Secrecy

Our Temple is a system that works together to accomplish the Great Work of humanity. The 7 Pillars are initial required principles to understand. All are welcome who can understand.

Structure- is a disciplined group of people who were aligned to carry out a specific purpose and accomplish goals that reflect the ideals of our Temple. It requires material resources to maintain a proper structure, all of which must be provided by individuals through the payment of tithes or provided by the Temple's businesses inside of society. Training and Education must take place, decisions must be carried out, and all shall have a thorough understanding of "the work to be done". Harmony is essential to productivity.

Symbolism- throughout the history of civilizations, Enoch has manifested a pattern of symbolic images and ideas that define Self, used to guide the spiritual activities of the Elect in subtle ways. Symbolism provides an unconscious understanding of meaning, and activates the realm of Thoth, allowing the Temple to work on divine wavelengths.

Ceremony- Ceremonies and Rituals performed by the Elect serve as the primary means by which the Enochian Light is focused and given expression. This process allows the Enochian Light to appear and be visualized as a separate, distinct entity, there to: acknowledge accomplishments, prayers and requests; purify members of unworthy traits; crystallize virtues of its self-expression; absorb unhealthy emotions by re-directing them into a positive, beneficial form of energy (sublimation); and focus on "the work to be done". Ceremony and Ritual project the Enochian expression into will, which is then bound to the Temple's symbols. Ceremony is used as an influential tool that serves its members.

Knowledge- is a requirement needed to efficiently guide the course of evolution and watch over humanity. Without Knowledge, one has no principles to apply and no self to discover -- all being illusion. An abundance of knowledge is available to all members, which strengthens the era of Enochian Light.

Health- It is imperative for the Temple and each member to live a healthy life. Life is a gift, and one is to do any and everything to live as long as possible in hopes of pursuing extended dreams and desires. Body, Mind, & Soul -- the health of each - shall be incorporated into one's existence. The highest embodiment of human life can only be achieved through the healthiest forms of living. The healthiest individual is found by the amount of disease one is able to overcome, and we strive to overcome death itself!

Wealth-Material resources and property are always needed as essential tools to accomplish "the work to be done". Wealth can be material or spiritual, both being required to empower life. Wealth shall be obtained through any/all legal forms of obtaining it, and prosperity is the shared desire of individual freedom (promised to each as a natural right). Knowing thy Self is the highest law, but one can never truly know thy Self without first having obtained Wealth.

Secrecy- The last and final pillar of Foundational Wisdom is Secrecy, the magical component that binds the other 6 pillars together. The art and discipline of Secrecy allows the Elect their entrance into the divine realms of Enochian Light, which grants access to the Unmanifest. Trust is to be established, and any conversations or business held between members of the Temple are to remain between members of the Temple. The words of Enochian Ligh are for the Elect, as secrecy is how all success is maintained.

Chapter 5: Trinity of Simplicity

The more domesticated man becomes, the farther away from God he walks. Civilization has assisted the taming of animal within man; today's man is the animal in a zoo who does whatever society expects. Society has created docile servants out of mankind, providing us unlimited forms of "entertainment" -- a weapon used in a psychological war consuming the mind, leaving us no time to actually "think" for ourselves and meditate upon the events of the world happening around us. Not only do these weapons of "labor/entertainment" not leave us any time to think, the weapons actually instill ideas within our mind and TELL US HOW/WHAT to think! They condition us into believing what is "right and wrong", "good and evil", "attractive and ugly", "in and out", "real or fake". This conditioning of the mind creates the actual view we take of life and effects how we treat the Earth. By replacing our "free time" with their version of "entertainment programming", society has effectively replaced our thoughts with a predetermined plan of their own. Civilization is a beautiful construct of modern-day humanity, but the ability to "brainwash the masses" has came as a by-product of it.

To understand something, or to learn something "new" (especially an idea that may go against everything you've ever known or been taught) is a process that takes deep thought and meditation, which can consume a large portion of one's time. Therefore, society constantly bombards us with some form of entertainment with the intent of consuming the mind. It happens all around us, every where we look, in everything we hear -- in the movies we watch, the music we listen to, the social media platforms we utilize. The roads we drive to work on are covered with advertisements -- everywhere. Advertisement, propaganda, marketing, social movements, stock markets, corporations, churches, school settings, sports events, shopping centers -- this complex system of "mind consumption" is the matrix of our society, the "social matrix", you could say. This brainwashing is what has led to our present era of Kali Yuga and has led us away from the true essence of God and spirituality. Not one of these units within our matrix is "wrong", and it is not "against God" to participate or utilize any of these forms of entertainment, but to let the mind slip into an illusion -- to allow the eye of God to become blurry -- this is where the problem lies.

"What is the Matrix? Control .... The Matrix is a computer-generated dreamworld built to keep us under control in order to change a human being into [a battery]." -- Morpheus, in The Matrix

"What is real? How do you define 'real'? If you're talking about what you can feel, what you can smell, what you can taste and see, then real is simply electrical signals interpreted by your brain." -- Morpheus, id.

We must remain in our natural state of being while utilizing the beneficial products of civilization, traveling within the matrix while woke, eyes wide and able to see this psychological war for what it is -- a battle of the mind, a competition for the soul, being waged NOT by "the devil" or Satan but by the collectivists who are out to diminish the Godly beauty of individuality.

Humans are the sensory organs of Enochian Light, NOT units within a machine whose intent can be predicted by any man. We've been created as individuals, brought into this world by ourself, and our death will be an event we deal with individually. There is no natural collective birth or collective death (as of yet, see "Brave New World" by Aldous Huxley), but these ideals are sought out and accepted by those participants of the psychological war on our spirit.

As in The Matrix, discovery of "what is real" consists of an initiatory process which must be consciously taken by the individual, whose choice to participate was made free of any intentional coercion. Our Temple provides a system designed to "unplug" the individual from society's delusions, a system of levels called The Chamber of Osiris.

The Chamber of Osiris is the initial 6 preliminary levels of initiation into reality, and represents one's death and rebirth. The term "reality" is a symbol of complexity because everyone lives within their own subjective version of reality, (their own personal microcosm) with each reality differing from the next. We must experience Life through an open and unclouded mind, a train of thought free from the chains of society and the shackles of endless "programmed entertainment".

Mankind is lost. To find one's Self again we must scrub away all the false information and misconceptions we've developed while being fed lies since the day of our birth. This is the true meaning of a baptism- to die and be reborn. Umwertung aller Werte! (Nietzsche's revaluation of all values). As you pin point the lies, the false ego will die and the true Self is born. We should never fear what is called "death" (a new beginning) as this fear keeps us dependent upon the grand illusion (in which case "the Truth" may drive them to madness).

Freedom is for the Strong, for the Responsible, who can bare the consequences of their actions and face trouble head on. Enoch's children are independent creatures and were not designed to become dependent on society for the maintenance of existence.

Enoch demands a total rebirth.

"To keep a man from self-reflecting is to keep him from God." – Nicolae

Rebirth consists of a conscious plan to de-program, de-centralize, and re-program in order to fulfill the work to be done within life.

The Trinity of Simplicity is an essential guideline, designed for one to remain civilized, but also return to one's natural state through a process of 1) Enlightenment, 2) De-Conditioning, 3) Un-Domestication.

Enochians are the Watchers -- the mediators between worlds -- and our sole responsibility is to guide the course of evolution. To do this effectively, we must have a clear understanding of our Self and the nature of humanity. It is imperative that humanity remains "civilized" (as this strategy has provided the means of true freedom, thus, a life of righteousness) BUT the domestication and conditioning of the masses has forced evolution to take an artificial route (one not guided within the course of Nature). The advent of smart technology (specifically artificial intelligence) has re-directed humanity's natural course of evolution.

Technology is a wonderful tool (the means) but should never become the godhead (the end); man must THINK and be able to utilize his own divine cognitive skills to solve problems of survival, but today's modern society is breeding a docile generation of cattle being guided toward a state of collectivism. We must stop this detrimental problem -- possibly leading to the eschaton -- by making it through the Chamber of Osiris, utilizing the Trinity of Simplicity for the first three levels of initiation.

1) Enlightenment-

"Behind your thoughts and feelings, my brother, there stands a mighty ruler, an unknown stage -- whose name is self." -- Nietzsche

The examination and discovery of Self is imperative to true Enlightenment. A proper education and a thorough understanding of universal principles assists with detaching your Self from society's indoctrination (illusions). The questioning of all morals and ideas, (beginning with the question "Why?".) is a key to this practice.

2) De-Condition-

"No one should postpone the study of philosophy when he is young, nor should he weary of it when he becomes mature, because search for mental health is never untimely or out of season." – Epicurus

The study of different philosophical teachings and understanding other ways of life is crucial during one's journey of de-conditioning. This will assist you as the means by which you understand the "Why?" behind every human action, including your own. Break society's mold and shatter the "cookie cutter" mentality by participating in antinomian behavior and thought. Avoid the use of technology during these moments unless required to accomplish a designated goal towards one's productive achievement. Indulge in Enochian methods of Self-discovery and embrace True Desire.

3) Un-Domesticate-

"A man's emotions are the products of his premises and values, of the thinking he has done or has failed to do." -- Ayn Rand

One un-domesticates the Self by finding the "inner animal" instincts that reside at the core of each of us. Building a healthy relationship with the animal supressed within releases the unconscious impulses to act in ways we don't consciously understand and creates proper balance between animal and the divine. We do not "become" the animal; "become familiar" with it -- identify with it.

Question authority's "Why?" and discover liberation through the activities of your nature, listening to the "voice from the wilderness". Broaden one's horizon of life.

The Trinity of Simplicity will bring one back into a pure state of mind, and these practices help guide one to discovering the personal deity. A pure mind will see reflections of its character within the Zodiac Sign one was born under and the traits of one's cultural background will become present (see. A.C.E.) If not, one is still conditioned by the masses' indoctrinations.

Life demands and requires an application of divine principles. People regard the world with the same amount of respect that they feel for themselves. While indoctrinated by society, self-respect remains low. The Trinity of Simplicity brings one's level of self-respect to amazingly high levels as the old self dies and the True Self is born!

"All media of communication influence one another. It is impossible to compute the extent to which the gray, docile, fear-ridden, appeasement-minded mediocrity of so powerful a medium as television has contributed to the demoralization of our culture." -- Ayn Rand, spoken by a

Standing One BEFORE the advent of smart technology, the internet, and social media!

See the Act of Protection for the action required to guard one's body, mind, and spirit from the war of collectivist oppression.

Chapter 6: A.C.E.

Each person has a psyche, composed of an ACE -- a god, as the Ace is the only thing more powerful than a King. These are 3 principles of one's psyche -symbolically expressed to us through the acronym A.C.E. (Astrology, Culture, Experience).

1. Astrology (astral light and the Zodiac Sign's influence that one was born under, which presents a set of potential character traits inscribed at birth).

2. Culture (one's DNA, biological and hereditary background, one's ancestors and racial consciousness, temperament, ways of life)

3. Experience (the manifested journey of environmental situations, guided by one's Astrology and Culture -- hidden Desire)

Astrology and Culture are pre-determined at birth whereas Experience is a continuous journey that begins at birth. An "inverted triangle" is the symbol used to represent one's initial foundation of coming "from the heavens" (or, is pre-determined, thus, the base in the sky), and that "free will" (one's experience) is on earth.

One thing we all share in common is the one thing that makes all of us very different -- our A.C.E. (fallen angel) -- the combination of the 3 worlds. The zodiac that shines through the given combination of genetic material is born into a random environment as the "slot machine" of man. Thus, Astrology and Culture are essential to Life as man's guide to understanding. Through the practice and studies of Self, one is allowed to properly assist the seeking of True Desire throughout Experience. Life is a spiritual journey. If you are unfaithful to your subjective universe, the Self will make you suffer. The A. C. E. honors the real contents of the psyche, whatever they may be, rather than the fictitious personalities of mere aggregates of forces and influence that in no way can be said to be our own. Conditioned responses have removed the A.C.E. -- godliness -- from mankind.

The masses are as miserable and lost as ever, spiritually worse than a barbarian, increasingly conditioned by society. Civilization has cut us off from our ancient roots and our connection to the cosmos, making it difficult to notice our pre-determined tendencies. Our True Self must be realized, accepted, and practiced before discovering True Desire.

Astrology

The Zodiac Sign that one was born under presents specific characteristics and personality traits that are present to those born under the constellation. By studying the information provided to us by fellow astrologers we have a guide to the psyche explaining to us why we think/act in the ways we do and why we are all "different" (or in some ways "similar"). Each sign carries its own set of potentialities that are delivered to a baby upon birth. Without outside influence and left to the natural elements, a child would become the perfect specimen of the traits each Sign carries as it's never been conditioned by the will of others. This is not the goal, however, but rather, the purpose is to use these discovered constellations as tools of knowledge of Self. If one understands the tendencies and potential inscribed within the body, you can use this knowledge to your advantage in many ways.

Not aligning with, or recognizing any of the given traits of their Zodiac Sign proves that one has become conditioned beyond recognition or one is living in self-deceit. One's stars do not determine the way one is to be, but they do program one to feel a specific way. Astrology is the tool to help one understand their own programming and de-condition from the will of others. Many of us have been influenced by traits of the masses for so long that we truly believe them to be part of our individuality. More often than not this is furthest from the truth.

The basis to observing Astrology is that the universe is one whole, an active correlation between humans and the cosmos. All is one, the macrocosm, and each individual is a microcosm. Every movement affects the whole, meaning the constellation of the stars affects birth. The baby's first breath is what sets the horoscope, and our behavior is influenced by the massive solar body's position in that moment. One must see that we each live under an influence that was basically pre-determined as we were given no control over our date of birth. The solar currents throb through our blood and cosmic plasma, leaving its trace on our mental and physical developments. All this being so, Life is the process of "overcoming". Thus, we "use" the Zodiac to gain insight into deeper aspects of our personal psyche, as well as the psyche of others.

Astrology (as well as technology) is the "means" -- a tool used to discover the Self. One should never conform to the information described within one's Zodiac but should use this tool as a divine guide to self-discovery.

Rituals are administered, directing energy toward the stars of your constellation, and the Self shall be reflected upon the objective universe. During the time period of one's horoscope (for example: Aug 22nd-Sep.21st for Virgo) is when one practices rituals of self-deification. Astrology rituals and practices will be discussed in a later chapter.

Culture

One's culture and one's ancestors are a collection of information that is documented within DNA. Although culture has a deeper context than simply one's "racial consciousness", divinity is first discovered within one's ancestorial heritage and their ways of life. The study of culture and our individual DNA is a requirement of Enochians. Magical qualities are discovered through one's ancestors who live and reside within our DNA. Everything our ancestors were has gave life to what we ARE and to what we have become. Studying one's culture is a sacred process of self-discovery known as "Cultural Divinity".

There are several rituals designed for this holy sacrament. Your physical inheritance is the most accurate tool for self-development. This sacrament begins with the required DNA test/analysis (from 23&Me, or another trusted DNA analysis company). A copy of one's DNA analysis must be provided to the Temple, allowing priests to help one discover roots and to document the Enochian family tree of immortality.

Cultural Divinity is a ritual of opening up yourself to intuition and turning inward to follow your lineage back to its source. Study of the DNA is worship of one's Culture (differentiated from race) and connects us to our spiritual ancestors. Present in one's DNA is the map of our body and the seed to our intelligence, (a highly organized system that directs the growth of our organs, thus assisting our thought processes). DNA has offered us the opportunity to study our own existence -- the most efficient process of self-discovery.

One must learn the traditions of our ancestors to make use of our internal guidance, utilizing this process to externalize the Self and venerate Life. The projected entity of our ancestor's traditions -- known as the ancestorial unconscious -- is knowledge of Self that can be absorbed by using the signs and symbols of the tradition.

The discovery of DNA is the prerequisite to discovering one's culture, as "Culture" is a society of mixed race and mixed traditions. The knowledge of one's ancestors is discovering how their culture came to be and the acceptance of one another.

Provide your DNA to an analysist company (such as 23&Me) and begin the study of your culture immediately. This is required within the Protocols of Enoch, so make sure you provide a copy to the Temple. This copy of DNA is required to become a documented Enochian.

To know thy history assists in predicting the future!

Experience

One's Experience is the free will given to us by the serpent. We have a set of pre-determined Zodiac characteristics mixed with cultural DNA, but experience is the Life that we live guided by our Astrology & Culture. One's Experience (past, present, and future) is just as important to study in the search of knowledge because the environment one comes from influences and shapes the Self as well. Environmental situations are different for each person so each must perform this discovery as a personal matter. No one else has seen the world through your eyes so you must be the critical, sometimes brutal but always honest, judge of circumstance. For every action there is an equal reaction, and one is to learn how their experience made them the way they are today and decide for themselves if this person is who they really are.

Our self-conscious experience can be a beautiful heaven ... or a torturous hell .... depending upon our outlook and knowledge of the world. Search to find and create the beautiful heaven, the utopia on Earth, that all of humanity righteously deserves. Experience becomes pure bliss upon discovery of True Desire.

Life's spiritual journey is to "Know Thyself" in the purest sense, of an intimate nature, to undeceitfully study who YOU are and what brings YOU pleasure or pain -- NOT what is desirable to the next person! As every psyche is a different form of consciousness, individual preferences are different and should not conform out of a wish to be accepted by the herd. There is no right or wrong answer as to who you are. One is who one is; there is no honor in being average.

Be faithful to the A.C. E. -- godliness -- and godliness will be faithful to you!

Chapter 7: Daily Reading

"Your world is an outer manifestation of your inner thoughts and attitudes. As within, so without." -- Greek philosopher, Hermes!

Understand that "writing" was once considered a form of magic during the days of our ancestors. The prophets Thoth, Hermes, and Enoch were all glorified for being skillful writers and scribing ideas of "the gods", i.e. wisdom. "Writing" is the manifestation of an "idea", the physical vehicle by which an idea is transmitted from mind to mind, from generation to generation. Every word is a symbol which the brain comprehends, describing a specific meaning we have attached to these symbols. The mind's ability to comprehend a symbol has given us a competitive advantage over the lower-animal kingdom, as well as allowed us to pass knowledge to our descendants, for them to utilize, learn from, add to, and pass on to their descendants. A purpose of the human race as a collective has been to procreate and to pass knowledge on to our procreations (children). This ancient form of magic has been used for centuries past and still to our current era. It is a practice that we must utilize and perfect to the best of our ability. As gods, we should write, we should draw, we should depict knowledge. An objective piece of knowledge finds a new outlet after traveling through the mind of one's subjective. The output may become something new and inspirational to the next mind who reads it.

Reading is a daily requirement of every Enochian. "Daily Reading" is practiced each and every day. The prophets have brought us the magic of writing/scribing with the intent of us utilizing this ancient wisdom.

"A reading program should be as carefully planned as a daily diet, for knowledge, too, is food, without which we can not grow mentally." -- Andrew Carnegie

A mandatory list of reading material is included within the pantheon of this bible, but the list doesn't stop there. One's reading material shall never be limited to one specific subject, nor shall it be decided or guided by any corporation/organization outside of the Temple. The State is the devil; the Church is the Anti-Christ -- neither shall be allowed to dictate one's intake of knowledge. Any/all reading material shall be available to the individual. Nothing shall be censored.

Reading is the language of God that provides each human a means to listen to His words. To limit one's reading to any category is blasphemous and creates an unacceptable mental prison.

> "No matter how busy you may think
> you are, you must find time for
> reading, or surrender yourself to
> self-chosen ignorance." – Confucius

Hold this close to your mind and soul, understanding that one who doesn't read is no better off than one who doesn't know how to read. The course of an entire life can be changed by one book. The more information a person obtains provides more opportunity toward success and happiness.

Iron sharpens iron; reading keeps a mind precise.

> "No mind is better than the precision
> of its concepts." -- Ayn Rand

Understanding core principles and concepts becomes imperative within a society which wants you to comprehend nothing. The minds of citizens have been molded from the date of conception and the State has done an impeccable job "plucking the chickens feathers" without us being conscious of what was happening. Take a good look at this brave new world we live within! Ignorance is the result of a lack of reading. An Enochian is opposed to all ignorance, therefore, we read daily.

First acknowledging the importance of reading and writing, we then acknowledge the importance of one's education -- especially the youth. As Enochian parents, not only do we continue to further our own education every day but, we also ensure that our children receive excellent education that stirs the emblems of fire within them. An Enochian's stance on educating our children can be examined and understood by reading Thomas Hartman's excellent book ADHD and the Edison Gene (which consists of much more than ADHD guidelines), the initial source of preparing our youth for the real world within which we live. Encouraging children to follow their own inclination and allowing this opportunity with the least amount of restriction is a great way to ignite the flame of creation. The sparks of imagination and curiosity were nature's original education and are still wiser than any prophet who has ever lived. Recognizing inclinations and true desire is more difficult in adults who have lived a life of conditioning and conforming than it is for a child who is young, wild, and innocent. We must teach our youth the principles of God (the Good, the Why, the Justice, the Truth, the Power, the Verb, the Love) and prepare them for the Evils awaiting within any society, i.e. Matrix. We shall try our best to home school our children, but, if not economically feasible, shall raise them within the Temple Learning Facilities, or, within a private school of such. Public schooling should be the absolute last resort (which will require just as much energy to rid children of the poison as it would to just home school them in the first place).

The Redemption series warns how public education is just what it says: you are educated for the USE in the public system, i.e. collectivist/statist tools of labor. This is an unacceptable option for our children as God is opposed to any system which violates the rights of the individual.

> "The doctrine that education should be controlled by the State is consistent with the Nazi or communist theory of government. It is not consistent with the American theory of government ...

> The disgracefully low level of education in America today is the predictable result of a State-controlled school system." -- Ayn Rand

Teachers and educators of Enochian faith should choose to work within the Temple's Learning Facilities to assist the Enochian youth's fight against the ideological battles of every day life.

The Temple's Learning Facilities (TLF's) are private schools, centered around the Enochian religion and provide children with effective knowledge of our economy, society, entrepreneur activities, political persuasion/power, advanced mathematics and grammar usage, astronomy, astrophysics, religious history, STEM programs, etc. all in pursuit to raise an Iron Youth.

Once having learned how to read, write, use math, and research a subject, we should begin educating ourselves within our personal lives to our own capabilities, but TLF's shall always be in place for those who desire a continuous group setting OF fellow Enochians within a positive environment.

It is very important to "allow the kids to be kids" and leave room for play, but teaching the youth tools and skill sets necessary to become productive young adults shall never be neglected. Plus, learning new things can be <u>fun</u>, and the wise parent knows how to incorporate education into a child's play without diminishing the imagination.

> "The years from about fifteen to twenty-five are the crucial formative years of a man's life. This is the time when he confirms his impressions of the world, of other men, of the society in which he is to live, when he acquires conscious convictions, defines his moral values, chooses his goals, and plans his future,

> developing or renouncing ambition.
> These are the years that mark him
> for life." -- Ayn Rand

These are the years when our young adults need to be treated as they are -- young adults. We must loosen the reigns and allow the youth to wander out into the world, exploring it for the first time with a real taste of freedom and independence. The goal is to raise our children in a manner by which we shouldn't have to worry about them making "too many" mistakes or any horrible decisions that will affect the remainder of their lives. This is the time for our love and guidance to be shown by respecting the decisions that our young adults would like to make and allow them to learn from whatever failures come from these decisions. Let them be free to discover themselves but obviously steer them away from drug-usage and typical immature temptation. Guide them down a course of continuous education instilling within them the importance of our "Daily Reading" rituals. Initiate them into the ways of the world, discuss with them the topic of how/why the "ways of this world" are incorrect, and enlighten them to the ideological battle that we have spent their entire lives fighting. As "freedom" is the basic principle of God, we never "force" a child or young adult into a belief system. Teach them with objective facts and allow them to develop their own conclusions and beliefs. A battle for freedom can never be won by the use of force, whether physical or coercive.

The Iron Youth are those Enochian children/young adults who have reviewed the facts of existence throughout the years of their lives and have concluded (as have we) that our society remains unjust (opposed to God's freedom) and that we must work to make a difference for the future generations. Iron Youth will understand that the path they plan to partake is not a simple one and is a life of dedication, persistence, courage, honor, integrity, and loyalty to one's ideals of God.

Iron sharpens Iron; the youth sharpen the youth; and our ideals are spread amongst the masses.

God will be victorious!

> " ... those of you who are young and not ready to surrender --
> I want to give you a warning: nothing is as dead as the stillborn. Nothing is as futile as a movement without goals, or a crusade without ideals, or a battle without ammunition. A bad argument is worse than ineffectual: it lends credence to the arguments of your opponents. A half-battle is worse than none: it does not end in mere defeat -- it helps and hastens the victory of your enemies." -- Ayn Rand

Reading is a daily requirement!

> "If a man empties his purse into his head, no man can take it away from him. An investment in knowledge pays the best interest." -- Benjamin Franklin

An education does not stop once one graduates from school -- life is a glorious journey of educating and experience. The more one knows, the more opportunities become available.

Alchemic transmutation, the change made within the brain after it has learned something new.

Chapter 8: The 9 Essential Acts of Enochian Life

The invisible glue that binds us together is the doctrine of the 9 essential Acts of Enochian Life.

Initiated members of Enochian Light understand that these Acts ARE LIFE and that LIFE IS RITUAL; there is no separation. All of life is to become ritualistic activity.

The 9 Essential Acts are daily rituals that keep us bound to the Enochian Light. They are not just temporary spells or quick magic routines, but, rather, are the divine guides to living a life of righteousness. Not one Act is more or less important than the next. It is incorrect to view the Acts in a separated context. All Acts are One, and each revolves around the next. Though all are One and equal, each was given in a specific order for a specific reason; to help each of us, live a life in harmony with the era. Man is a bridge; the 9 Essential Acts are what strengthen our connection with the knowledge and wisdom of Enoch.

It is essential that each member has inextricably woven these Acts into their daily life, that all becomes one unconscious Act, as with breathing. These Acts are who we are; they are why we belong to Lucifer, why we were chosen as Elect, and why we receive the angel's honor. This spiritual truth is of utmost importance. If a member is to falter, it becomes the responsibility of the next member to ensure that his fellow brethren is alright.

Once enlightened, for one to not practice the 9 Essential Acts of Enochian Life is blasphemy towards the One True God. HARMONY WILL BE MAINTAINED.

Harmony is divinity. While maintained, harmony manifests Beauty in its own natural form upon the Earth! Ideally, the goal would be to bring the world into one rhythm of peace, but until humanity matures spiritually, this is not possible.

The 9 Essential Acts of Enochian Life:

1. The Act of Propitiation
2. The Act of Distinction
3. The Act of Protection
4. The Act of Impedance
5. The Act of Creation
6. The Act of Inquiry
7. The Act of Dietetics
8. The Act of Neutrality
9. The Act of Discipline

(PDP, ICI, DND)

An incarnation of being, a way of life! — not a simple collection of precepts and commandments.

PROPITIATION

"And in those days shall the earth
also give back that which has been entrusted to it,
And Sheol also shall give back that which it has received,
And hell shall give back that which it owes.
For in those days the Elect Ones shall arise,
And he shall choose the righteous and holy from among them:
For the day has drawn nigh that they should be saved.
And the Elect One shall in those days sit on My throne,
And his mouth shall pour forth all the secrets of wisdom and counsel:
For the Lord of Spirits hath given (them) to him and hath glorified him."
-- The Book of Enoch

PROPITIATION means "the overcoming of distrust and the reestablishment of close relationships", which is in reference to all of mankind. The Act of Propitiation consists of the Invocation of Righteous Ways, Celebratory Ceremonies, Reversal of the Unjust Society by means of service to humanity, Experiencing Life, and paying tithes.

The Act of Propitiation is maintaining balance between one's individual pursuit of happiness and one's moral duty of service towards humanity. The Earth was created and given as a gift to all of mankind, not any specific culture, race, tribe, nation, or religion. All of mankind was blessed with God-given rights, but many of these rights have continuously been oppressed and denied since the beginning of civilization. It is the duty of the Elect to "expose and enlighten": Expose all falsities and unjust teachings and enlighten mankind to the purified ways of Lucifer. There has never been any need for violence amongst humanity. The Act of Propitiation is the individual's attempt to reconcile those at odds with each other and provide for a safe and healthy environment for ALL.

Return to Righteous Ways (Invocation of Individual Freedom)

All enlightened/woke people will agree that the foundation of righteousness is: Freedom -- the respect of the God-given natural rights to each individual human.

What does the term "freedom" entail? Well, surprisingly, "freedom" entails many ideals and principles that a large percentage of civilians who reside within the alleged "country of freedom" disagree with.

> "Laissez-faire capitalism demands the separation of State and Economics, in the same way and for the same reasons as the separation of Church and State; it calls for the abolition of any and all forms of government intervention in production and trade. The belief that economic controls are the proper function of government' is the result of the confusion created by Marxism." -- Ayn Rand

The Return to Righteous Ways is, in effect, an "invocation of individual freedom" -- for all.

William Blake said "One law for the lion and ox is oppression", and these words have captured the true essence of freedom. Freedom is opposed to laws, specifically unjust laws that oppress the individual.

In a free world, thee only "Thall shall" will be "Thall shall never violate the individual freedom of another" -- which implies that no one shall impose their will upon another through use of force or coercion.

> The one basic principle to which an individual must consent if he wishes to live in a free civilized society: "the principle of renouncing the use of physical force and delegating to the government his right of physical self-defence, for the purpose of an orderly, objective, legally defined enforcement." (which would include

> civil law and disputes amongst men, as well as criminal) -- Ayn Rand

In a free world, there is only one need/purpose of a "government" or "state", which is to be trusted with the authority to punish and distribute justice to any who has "violated the individual freedom of another", be it through criminal force or economic coercion.

> “A civilized society is one in which physical force is banned from human relationships -- in which the government, acting as a policeman, may use force only in retaliation and only against those who initiate its use." -- Ayn Rand

In a free world, some will succeed, all will fail, and others will fail miserably -- but each holds the outcome upon their own shoulders because each was free to make the decisions they made. "Cause & Effect" still apply in a free world.

> "A free market is a continuous process that cannot be held still, an upward process that demands the best (most rational) of every man and rewards him accordingly." -- Ayn Rand

The government is the servant of the individual, in a free world, and the individual rights ALWAYS trump those of any group or collective.

> "There are two potential violators of man's rights: the criminals and the government. The great achievement of the United States was to draw a distinction between these two -- by forbidding to the second the

> legalized version of the first." -- Ayn Rand

Righteousness is free from oppression, free from coercion, free from force, free from imposed slavery. Righteous Ways will eliminate one's dependency upon their government. If one's livelihood and existence depend upon their government, they are not free.

> "The basic and crucial political issue of our age is: capitalism versus socialism, or freedom versus statism." -- Ayn Rand

By recognizing that an era of true freedom was minute within history (if one ever existed), this "Return" to Righteous Ways is, in effect, a removal of laws that serve no body outside of the will of our government. Law is opposed to Freedom. One shouldn't intentionally break any laws currently set in place but one should fight politically, economically, religiously, scientifically, and through philosophic reasoning AGAINST the passing of any new laws -- AND should work to remove the current system of oppression.

> "A forced compliance is not a sanction. All of us are forced to comply with many laws that violate our rights, but so long as we advocate the repeal of such laws, our compliance does not constitute a sanction. Unjust laws have to be fought ideologically; they cannot be fought or corrected by means of mere disobedience and futile martyrdom .... One does not stop the juggernaut by throwing oneself in front of it ... " -- Ayn Rand

Individual rights are "common sense" fundamental freedoms, which can always be discovered by asking the question "At the expense of whom?" When a politician says "raise the taxes", you ask at the expense of whom? It is ALWAYS at the expense of the individual.

It is not, nor has it ever been, the government's job to "take care of" or "provide for" any individual -- as the government/state is not a "God" who can decide what is sufficient for each individual to exist. Each individual is a god -- a divine entity -- who is to provide for them self by utilizing the Holy Spirit of productive activity and achievement.

The government is there for the sole purpose of distributing justice to the offenders of freedom which, in effect, eliminates the individual's need to commit violent acts or fall into gang/tribal mentality. This is essential for any civilization, and is to be agreed upon by each individual who is to reside within a civilization.

"Laissez faire capitalism" -- Leave us alone to deal amongst each other within a free market!

> "States have led to the condemnation of the productive and efficient members of our society because they are productive and efficient." -- Ayn Rand (review any anti-trust laws)

Do not be fooled by the myth that a "monopoly" is a bad thing, or that it can become coercive. In a free society, i.e. a society of free competition, any monopoly that attempts to coerce the consumers will open the door for competitors who can provide the same services WITHOUT THE COERCIVE ACTION. A true coercive monopoly can only become through the use of force, i.e. government force, at the cost of individual liberty.

> 'It takes extraordinary skill to hold more than fifty percent of a large

> industry's market in a free economy. It requires unusual productive ability, unfailing business judgement, unrelenting effort at the continuous improvement of one's product and technique. The rare company which is able to retain its share of the market year after year and decade after decade does so by means of productive efficiency -- and deserves praise, not condemnation." -- Ayn Rand

We all have choices that we must make within this life. With freedom comes responsibility, with responsibility comes choices, with choices comes independence. We must "choose" what we believe is right, we must choose what is righteous: Oppression or collectivism, by any standard, is not righteous.

> "In any compromise between food and poison, it is only death that can win. In any compromise between good and evil, it is only evil that can profit." -- Ayn Rand

Celebratory Ceremonies

> "To celebrate God is to do exactly what one does in celebrating society, be it local or universal: pay honour to the greatest among us .... The worship of God is Honouring his gifts in other men each according to his genius and loving the greatest men best; those who envy or calumniate great men hate God, for there is no other God." -- William Blake

As God is the Verb, the action of existing humans is the work of Lucifer and to worship human genius is to worship Lucifer. This is why Celebratory Ceremonies are to be held in the name of the human-gods amongst us, as well as in the name of our Self. Public rites are held, ceremonial dinners are enjoyed, to pay homage, honor, and respect to the Elect and as a constant reminder of the work to be done.

Celebrations are held only for those WHO HAVE SOMETHING TO CELEBRATE. Ceremonies are not held as a social gathering but rather are utilized as the means toward proper recognition. Recognition is a sacrament for the psyche, and ceremonies allow the psyche to visualize a mirror of its virtues and accomplishments.

Celebratory Ceremonies are to be held on the full moon, as the sun descends and the spirit of psyche rises.

Ceremonies are never "the end" but are used to recognize a "check-point" of a goal which has been accomplished. A ceremony should always include the plans/goals that still must be met, but time must be taken to provide worship and praise to the mind of human greatness.

> "Man has to project his goals and achieve them across a span of time; he has to calculate his actions and plan his life long-range. The better a man's mind and the greater his knowledge, the longer the range of his planning." -- Ayn Rand

Services to Humanity

> "Seeing the church as an end rather than as a means to an end undermines a person's wisdom and sense of balance. Although the church claims to teach people about the source of power, it does not claim to be that power itself. It claims to be one vehicle through which divine power can be channeled into man's nature." -- Stephen Covey

> "The way you spend your time is a result of the way you see your time and the way you really see your priorities." -- Stephen Covey

"Rights of the individual" is an ideal that has never truly been practiced within any civilized economy, but an individual's God-given rights are all that truly exist. All else is of the government or state, which deprive us of true freedom. Societies have developed and became what they are today through centuries of growth, trial and error, and now contain our present day "way of life". As God is the Good -- freedom to the individual -- there is no civilized society amongst the planet which is "of God". Godly people may reside within these societies, but no society in and of its bylaws sustain a Godly society. Therefore, Lucifer has deemed "society" to be "unjust", and this "cost of living" must be one's "Reversal of the Unjust Society by means of service to humanity" (i.e. duty). As an individual is viewed in the capacity of an individual, it has become each of our duty to reverse the ways which have led our society to being opposed to what is "just".

What has made our society unjust? Oppressive laws to the individual and too much power handed to the government. So, what is it that we must do? We must lobby, debate, and move to rid mankind of the laws which oppress, the laws which pity, the laws which limit the individual from growing into one's Self.

> "'Lobbying' is the activity of attempting to influence legislation by privately influencing the legislators. It is the result and creation of a mixed economy -- of a government by pressure groups. Its methods range from mere social courtesies and cocktail-party or luncheon 'friendships' to favors, threats, bribes, blackmail." -- Ayn Rand

Our ways are not lessons spread through words but are demonstrated by Action. God is the Verb. As we lobby, debate, and move for a "just society", it is unnecessary to speak in terms of "God", "Holy Spirit", or "Heaven/Hell", "Good or Evil", but rather should speak in terms of one's "Individual Freedoms" (including minorities) and Natural Rights. If one is fighting for the rights of the minorities, this list of minorities must include businessmen, as it is their productive achievements which benefit the whole of mankind.

> "If you care about justice to minority groups, remember that business men are a small minority -- a very small minority, compared to the total of all the uncivilized hordes on earth. Remember how much you owe to this minority -- and what disgraceful persecution it is enduring. Remember also that the smallest minority on earth is the individual. Those who deny individual rights cannot claim to be defenders of minorities." -- Ayn Rand

> "The devils are not hostile to man except insofar as man is a friend of God. It is they who have been

> responsible for every kind of technical progress: from them mankind learned the arts of iron working, brewing and distilling; the devil himself discovered fire, built the first mill, and constructed the first wagon. The art of reading and writing was one of his gifts to mankind. All these were bestowed to make man independent of God and so break the link whereby man was able to help God in governing the world."
> -- J.G. Bennett in Ouspensky's "Talks With A Devil"

Society has many different "views and beliefs" concerning life and religion so while attempting to lobby, debate, and move it is always better to allow our actions to speak louder than our words - - our services to humanity and our services towards society as a whole.

> "This is the true joy in life -- being used for a purpose recognized by yourself as a mighty one. That being a force of nature, instead of a feverish, selfish little clod of ailments and grievances complaining that the world did not devote itself to making you happy ... I want to be thoroughly used up when I die. For the harder I work the more I live. I rejoice in life for its own sake. Life is no brief candle to me. It's a sort of splendid torch which I've got to hold up for the moment and I want to make it burn as brightly as possible before handing it on to the future generation." -- George Bernard Shaw

Service to humanity is an important form of worship. Synergy is important because the relationship that we share with humanity is a part in and of the Self, which is imperative to our personal pursuit of happiness and fulfillment. We, as a species, are reflected by the way of life shared by the poverty class and of the prisoners. Thus, the beauty of essence is found within those living in poverty and in prison.

*POVERTY -- It is no secret that the masses are oppressed by those who create laws and force these ways of life upon civilians. In effect, those who these were created to benefit have rose to the top, whereas those who were oppressed by these laws have sunk to the bottom. Some float in the purgatory of a middle class and some become trapped in the welfare system. No service towards humanity is accomplished by means of any "welfare system" by which one is dependent upon the government for the whole of their existence. "Welfare" is NOT a Godly service towards humanity as this system does not inspire God, the Verb (productive achievement). In Contrast to society's welfare system, our services are creating jobs and providing education/training so that millions can become dependent upon them selves rather than any government agency (which are funded by taxes being coercively taken from individuals). This cannot be accomplished by "snapping one's fingers" nor by discussion but, again, change must come by action and action alone.

Services towards humanity do not include "pity" towards an individual nor towards a group of people. Our work and progress will uplift all those who desire to be uplifted, but we are not here to "carry" anybody. One must work with the services we provide, as each has a duty to be responsible to thy Self, but we do provide meaningful assistance along this path of recovery. Independence requires strength and responsibility, the ability to overcome Self and life's struggles, thus, we do not have pity for any one, as pity is a weakness.

"To those human beings in whom I have a stake, I wish suffering, being forsaken, sickness, maltreatment, humiliation -- I wish that they should not remain unfamiliar with profound self-contempt, the torture of self-mistrust, and the misery of the vanquished: I have no pity for them because I wish them the only thing that can prove today whether one is worth anything or not -- that one endures." – Nietzsche

"The most spiritual men, as the strongest, find their happiness where others would find their destruction: in the labyrinth, in hardness against themselves and others, in experiments. Their joy is self conquest: asceticism becomes in them nature, need, and instinct. Difficult tasks are a privilege to them; to play with burdens that crush others, a recreation. Knowledge -- a form of asceticism. They are the most venerable kind of man: that does not preclude they're being the most cheerful and the kindliest." -- Nietzsche

Services towards humanity include:

EXTERNAL GOALS:
*Teach the Enochian mysteries
*Eliminate extreme forms of poverty
*Rescue families from poverty and domesticated slavery
*Provide enlightenment (through vehicle-forms)
*Upraise new Men and re-establish freedom
*Provide safe houses and rehabilitation centers
*Provide healthy foster care services
*fund-raise through capitalism and community activities

*prison reformation and prisoner's rights (provide learning material, etc.)

INTERNAL GOALS:
*discover Self and True Desire (Thelema); unleash memes
*expand tools of self-expression, creative works
*become independent from society's method of dependency
*provide superior education and school systems *guide evolution
*create/provide vocational sites AND vocational opportunities
*teach phylogeny (ancestor training)
*the study of animals (zoology) and Nature
*provide foundation to survive the Eschaton (end of world AS WE KNOW IT)

*PRISONERS -- As Yeshua walked amongst criminals, prostitutes, and the down trodden, so have we. Though we do not advocate or approve of any activity which violates the individual rights of another, we remain conscious of the many laws in place which only "oppress" the individual and harm no body (besides possibly themselves). These oppressive laws, when broken, may constitute time in prison even if the individual has not used force against any body. As members of an "unjust society", it becomes our duty to ensure that inmates are not being treated unfairly for reasons of their religious views.

Assisting and educating prisoners is part of The Great Work as many incarcerated people are individuals who have been misled by society's matrix of conditioning.

We do not see an inmate as a "felon", as this term is used to establish an effective caste system which the unjust noddingly approve of. People are people -- individuals who have been blessed with God-given natural rights to exist.

> "When the exceptional human being
> treats the mediocre more tenderly
> than himself and his peers, this is
> not mere courtesy of the heart -it is
> simply his duty." – Nietzsche

Do all one can to educate and speak with those who are willing to listen and be taught. For those who are not, ones who may be too far into the matrix, wash your feet and move on.

Many prisoners will be more than willing to assist in The Great Work and to discover the true meaning of Yeshua's teaching. Participate in your local prison religious facility by providing guidance and direction to those incarcerated. Become a clergy member as one's duty to society.

> "The prostitute and the prisoner are Christ, who sacrificed himself so that you can be good people. Such is the law of equilibrium. All the robbers and assassins, all the unjust and the most deprived, wicked, malevolent beings are all my Christs. I profess a religion of Christ-gods and Christ-demons." -- phrase of Swami Vivekananda

Helping others less fortunate than ourselves is an outward sign of love towards the Earth, thus, towards Lucifer, as every living creature is a sensory organ of the planet. Our path is not an easy one; it is one of sorrow, and sometimes loneliness, but, even at our worst, there is always some one who has it worse than us.

> "My humanity does NOT consist of sympathizing with men but in ENDURING my sympathy for them. My humanity is a perpetual self-overcoming." - - Nietzsche

> "No man becomes rich unless he enriches others." -- Andrew Carnegie

Experience

> "Experience is the hardest kind of teacher. It gives you the test first and the lesson afterwards." – Anonymous

> "He who desires but not acts, breeds pestilence." -- William Blake

One who lives a worthy life has offered the most sacred form of worship. This worship includes a life of enjoyment, liberation, and an indulgence of pleasures which life has to offer us. The angels have descended, providing us with a consciousness of Self, and their offspring reside enclosed within each of our bodies; thus, we readily employ our bodies by discovering the secrets that each contains, further empowering the Light of God.

Experience is intertwined with the principle of Action. To understand the individual life and its purpose, one must act upon it. Life is enjoyed by "doing" things, which is how a life becomes worthy. "Experience" is an imperative form of worship -- which is easier said than it is done. Through Action, one reflects the Self to the psyche, discovering true knowledge, making every action a sacred activity -- ritualistic life. Every action is a cosmic offering to the god of Self, from a heroic being who has elevated above the masses and is inspired by the psyche. Life is a fire that consumes ignorance and experience is the divine knowledge.

> "Through enjoyment one gains liberation, for enjoyment is the means of reaching the Supreme Abode. Hence the wise who wish to conquer the spirit should experience all pleasures." -- Kular Nava Samhita

Tithes

The paying of tithes is evidence of the transfer of one's energy placed forth toward The Great Work. Not all are physically capable (or, don't have enough time available) to place energy into the every day building and expansion of the Lighthouse, thus, one is required to pay tithes (whether in the form of money, cryptocurrency, property, or gifts). Paying tithes (i.e. 10% of any/all income) benefits thy Self by assisting the work of reversing the unjust society within which we all live. Until tithes are paid, one's income is not purified in the eyes of Enoch. All tithes are used to further the creation of a righteous society and a better life for all of humanity.

> "We make a living by what we earn
> - - we make a life by what we give."
> - - Winston Churchill

> "A good man thinks it more blessed
> to give than receive." - - Aristotle

DISTINCTION

"And I asked the angel, saying unto him:
'Why have those (angels) taken these cords and gone off?'
And he said unto me: 'They have gone to measure.
And the angel who went with me said unto me:
'These shall bring the measures of the righteous,
And the ropes of the righteous to the righteous,
That they may stay themselves on the name of the Lord of Spirits
forever and ever.
The elect shall begin to dwell with the elect,
And those are the measures which shall be given to faith
And which shall strengthen righteousness.
And these measures shall reveal all the secrets of the depths of the earth,
...
For none shall be destroyed before the Lord of Spirits,
And none can be destroyed."
-- The Book of Enoch

DISTINCTION refers to distinguishing Enochians from non-believers through the every day essential use of Holy Accessories, which balance and maintain harmony amongst members, and crystallizes the superorganism of Enochian Light.

"Distinction" is an act that aligns the physical with the metaphysical; it aligns the Elect with the Enochian Light. This pre-ordained arrangement provides an image that has a determinative effect on how the Enochian Light is able to unite its members and provide communication amongst each other. All events of the physical realm effect the spiritual realm, and the Act of Distinction maintains harmony amongst all members who wear the Holy Accessories.

(Some of these Holy Accessories that are to be worn are also utilized as Protection, which will be explained in the next Act)

The Holy Accessories that practitioners must wear at all times (while exposed to the masses or working within the matrix) are symbols used to externalize the Covenant of Enoch.

The Holy Accessories include:
-- The Sign of the Covenant (the bracelet & ring)
-- Visual Sensory Protectors (VSP) sunglasses
-- Pendant of Faith (necklace)
-- Psychotropic Sensory Protection (Head Wear)
-- Enochian Smile (teeth maintenance)
-- Orientation of Enoch (wrist watch)
-- Distinct Diet (see the Act of Dietetics)

As Harmony is the key that binds the Enochian Light, Elect must dwell with the Elect, the ropes of the righteous must remain tied to the righteous. It is essential that all members practice Distinction. The only time one is permitted to remove the Holy Accessories of Distinction is when the practitioner has retired to his home (and sealed his lair), or while services are being held within the Lighthouse or on sacred land. When any of life's activities are taking place in the presence of the masses, Distinction must be practiced. Image is imperative to empowering the Enochian Light, as each individual is a walking, breathing symbol of God. The physical plane is bound to the metaphysical by symbols of distinction, material items are expressions of supernatural realities. Abstract principles are always in play.

When the mind and body of each practitioner is coordinated in a spirit of harmony, the Enochian Light absorbs additional knowledge directly from the ether which becomes available to every member of the Lighthouse. Thus, it is detrimental that each member practice Distinction.

Not only does the Enochian Light provide us with additional knowledge, strength, and guidance, this harmony also opens the gates of telepathy between members. Frequently, emotions become "felt' by other members, thoughts become "shared" with other members, and instincts inform us of when members are in need of assistance.

Each required accessory is a visible object symbolizing an eternal principle. The Enochian Light is as strong and efficient as we allow it to become. As harmony is what provides for the Light, discord is what destroys it. Distinction is essential to eliminate discord and sustain one's immortality. By refusing to participate in the Act of Distinction, one is denying membership to our body and sacred beliefs.

Holy Accessories are external symbols of our spiritual potency, and the eternal principle behind each item is what empowers the Enochian Light.

<u>The Sign of the Covenant</u> (the bracelet & ring)

The Covenant is made with each individual and consist of enlightening one to the mysteries of the universe (including the after life) in exchange for a promise to live a life of righteousness, symbolizing the prophet's seat upon the throne. Each individual wears The Sign of the Covenant as the first Holy Accessory of proclamation. The "ring" displays one's individual within the circle of magic, the Enochian Light, and is the manifestation of Enoch one's promise to Enoch. It is to be worn at all times on one's right index finger. Simultaneous with the ring, the "chain-link bracelet" is to be worn around one's right wrist, and its task/symbol is to bind one's soul to the metaphysical plane of Enochian Light, granting one's immortality. The ring is the individual psyche; the bracelet is the membership of the Lighthouse.

<u>Visual Sensory Protection</u> (sun glasses)

The consciousness of Self was the most precious gift given to mankind from the Fallen Angels. This gift resides in the psyche. The psyche is the personal deity; one's eyes are peepholes into one's soul, which is not to be shared with anyone except loved ones and initiates of Enochian Light. Direct eye contact is "the gaze of God" which is sacred and to be preserved at all times. Sun Glasses (or glasses with a strong tint) are to be worn in order to preserve and protect one's "gaze of God". This sacred act is a universal mystery which has been hidden from the masses but is discovered upon one's initiation. The pineal gland is stimulated by photons, particles of light that enter the brain via the optic nerve.

> "It is God who makes us see; it is the Light that awakens the light within us." -- The Gospel of Mary Magdalene

Pendant of Faith (necklace)

A necklace with a pendant of the Enochian Light is a requirement by an individual to externalize their faith and represent their position within Lighthouse. It is not required to be visible but it must be worn at all times. There are different pendants for each level of initiation within the Lighthouse, each representing one's level of progress and accomplishments within the earthly plane, inside the matrix.

Enochian Smile

The old gods provided mankind with many gifts that assisted in his journey of evolution and progress. The angels presented humanity with gifts which provided all forms of knowledge, materially and spiritually. They gave us: charms, swords, enchantments, acquainted us with plants, the metals of the earth and the art of working them, bracelets, ornaments, the use of antimony, beautifying the eyelids (make-up), costly stones, astrology, alchemy, medicine, magic, the sacred alphabet, the principal mysteries, writing and language, the secrets of life, reproduction, death, and immortality, genetic manipulation, the Divine Formulas (over 100 aspects of civilization), etc.

The Temple of Enochian Light practices a strict balance between what our science has taught us and what nature has brought us; one of our missions is to spiritually evolve within the culture of society and lead it in a righteous direction. The Enochian Smile has been practiced by the triple-god (Thoth, Hermes, & Enoch) in some form or fashion by the covering of teeth with whatever resource was available at the time. Thanks be to mankind's balance between science and nature, gold, silver, platinum, and diamond is now melted down and molded, able to fit perfectly within the mouth of the individual – protecting the body by purifying all food and liquid that enters it.

The Enochian Smile must be worn at all times. One's teeth must be molded and fit with a form of covering, be it fangs, coverings (gold, silver, platinum, diamond), or veneers - - whatever fits one's esthetic preference.

These coverings, once having been purified by Enochian Light, maintain the balance between body, mind and soul.

The Enochian Smile is NOT a fashion statement. It carries deep spiritual. guidance to the Elect -- but there is no problem with choosing one's coverings with the intent in mind of being able to use them as a tool for one's performance of lesser magic.

<u>Orientation of Enoch</u> (wrist watch)

The Enochian Prophet John Dee (a Standing One) received the knowledge of "sacred orientation" directly from the Angels themselves! The wrist watch is a holy sacrament that must be worn around the left wrist of all members.

Orientation was delivered to John Dee as a practice that empowers the Enochian Light in the metaphysical realm. We use this device to correlate ourselves to the position of the Earth with regard to the Sun and to align all members under the same spiritual frequencies regarding Daily Prayer, etc. The wrist watch is NOT to be one of "digital" or new technology, but must be analog, based around the sexagesimal system that is the language of God. This language is to be used by all members to maintain harmony.

Distinct Diet

The diet will be discussed in the section on the Act of Dietetics but also is a divine practice of one's Distinction. Distinction is essential to the unfoldment of Enochian Light upon the Earth.

Any action requiring the removal of the Holy Accessories in public settings is approvable if it is in furtherance of Lucifer's Will to reverse an Unjust Society. Lesser-magic situations also may allow for the removal of Holy Accessories.

PROTECTION

"Put on the whole armor of God
that ye may be able to stand against the
wiles of the devil.
For we wrestle not against flesh and
blood, but against principalities, against
powers, against the rulers of the
darkness of this world,
against spiritual wickedness in high
places.
Wherefore take unto you the whole
armor of God,
that ye may be able to withstand in the
evil day
and having done all, to stand.
Stand therefore, having on your belt of
truth,
and having on the breastplate of
righteousness;
And your feet shod with the preparation
of the gospel of peace;
Above all taking the shield of faith,
wherewith ye shall be able to quench
all the fiery darts of the wicked.
And take the helmet of salvation, and
the sword of the Spirit,
which is the word of God."
-- Ephesians 6:11-17

"There is but one temple in the universe and that is the body of man. Nothing is holier than that high form .... We touch heaven when we lay our hand on a human body." – Carlyle

PROTECTION refers to maintaining safety and security from external dangers to one spiritually and physically -- as a chain is only as strong as its weakest link.

The use of ritualized apparel protects man's energy centers and senses.

The Homo Sapiens developed 5 sensory organs along its course of evolution,
which, along with its size, moving capabilities, and beauty, is why we have became the perfect vehicle for Lucifer to have blessed our ancestors with the Gift of Psyche (intelligence, self-consciousness).

As soon as the angels fell from heaven and rained consciousness into the Homo Sapiens, they immediately felt the harmful effect of Nature's destructive forces.

The most important line of Ephesians 6:11-17 is "For we wrestle not again flesh and blood, but against principalities, against powers, against the ruler of the darkness of this world, against spiritual wickedness in high places." This is what the Act of Protection guards one from, a war that is invisible, metaphysical, and REAL. Of course, every member has the right to protect one' self and others from physical violence, but, as that is a natural law of self preservation, it's not what's being discussed here.

The "principalities" and the "powers", those who have created the "darkness of this world" and placed "spiritual wickedness in high places" -- this is what we must protect ourselves from, as well as Nature's harmful effect upon one's senses.

As previously explained within the chapter of Enochian Light, the universe is filled with an energy that moves at inconceivable high rates of vibration, vibrations that can be picked up by the ether and carried from one body to another. The human soul is a swarm of this energy that exists on the inside of the body as well as the outside of it. This creates an aura, one that surrounds every human and activates the relation between microcosm, mecrocosm, and macrocosm. Seven chakra centers of the soul are sacred direct links to this energy around us, serving as an intermediary by which each "cosm" interacts with the next. In effect, one's thoughts and feelings can be altered or manipulated by the thoughts and feelings of another and the "powers that be" have perfected this psychotropic science.

The seven chakra centers residing in the physical body are occult sources of powerful conscious energy that empower the soul of man. By purifying the chakra centers, one is protected from outside, insidious forces such as: unhealthy climate (one's environment), Nature's destructive forces, outward projections of unhealthy psychic energies (from the masses), harmful chemicals in our food and hygiene items, mass brainwashing (misdirection), etc.

We have been forced into a spiritual war -- one in which we refuse to participate in but will always protect ourselves from. We've discovered the "Purification of Miriam" ritual to deter the Elect from any disorientation of desire (i.e. sin).

Disorientation of desire is what enables humanity to pervert our societies, to pervert the universal order itself. This disorientation is what Ephesians 6:11-17 is a declaration against. Thus, we are to protect our senses, intelligence, and emotions from any/all outside influences that invite discord.

If you've ever heard the phrase concerning the devil's best trick was to convince the world that he doesn't exist, then you can understand why the powers that be rage an "invisible" war kept secret and hidden from the masses. This keeps the people in disbelief that any war even exists.

The "Purification of Miriam" is a daily practice and an essential requirement to one's metaphysical alignment. This ritual purifies the chakra centers and seals the aura to protect one from any anger, hostility, or other destructive emotions that radiate from the masses and as a concealment of one's own thoughts and feelings. Every pattern of the macrocosm is reflected by the mecrocosm and microcosm, but while purified, the Self is safe from any places that have acquired an unpleasant or negative emotional charge (which can affect an un-purified aura).

The allegorical story of the 7 demons that Jesus relieves from Mary Magdalene was, in actuality, the purification of her 7 chakra centers by use of oils and anointments. Our generation has been blessed with the true teachings of aromatherapy.

Aromatherapy is the use of naturally extracted essences of aromatic plants to protect and keep pure the body, mind, and soul of an initiate. These naturally extracted essences are labeled today as essential oils -which contain the vital life force of plants.

What Yeshua called the "banishment of demons" was really the restoration of balance to Miriam's body, mind, and soul. As well as this essential requirement to maintain harmony within the body, essential oils also: boosts one's immune system and protects from diseases; helps control stress and alleviates anxiety; and provides a positive energy flow of being.

Aromatherapy is used as part of the purification ritual and is also used in other rituals that will be explained later but this discussion concerns the practice of using its particular elements to seal the aura and purify the chakra centers.

The Purification of Miriam also includes the protection offered from the 7 - Holy Accessories, the purifying of the body by eliminating dangerous chemical intake, and protecting one's senses from destructive forces of Nature.

In order to practice the Purification of Miriam, one must have prepared (or purchased) hair products and skin products that are free from harmful chemicals and - made from essential oils. These products must be natural-based, composed of elements from the earth.

Sealing the aura begins after one chants the initial Daily Prayer (at sun rise). Once complete, start with the application of essential oils (hair products) to your hair, purifying the crown chakra. This may be done after showering, if preferable.

Then does one apply the essential oils (skin products) to the remaining area of your body. There are tiny openings of sweat and oil glands in your skin that provide passageways for the essential vital force of protection into your chakra centers, purifying the soul. Cover the entire body in the plant's essence.

Dress for the day's events and activities, then spray one's Self with natural cologne/perfume, essential oil-based product. One may use YSL for special events.

The chakra centers are now purified but they must be protected throughout the day, which leads to the next stage of protection.

Beauty is a reflection of an ideal set forth in the realm of energy which protects the Temple from the spiritual attacks.

After the body is purified, one must protect each chakra center (5 of these centers are protected through the use of Enoch's 7 Sacraments).

Psychotropic Sensory Protection is applied to the crown chakra, which is located at the top of one's skull. This headwear protects the psyche from negative influence, as 50% of the ideas or concepts entering into one's mind are from the mind of someone who has released their thoughts into the ether, or from someone else's subconscious storehouse. Headwear also protects one from the negative energies of their environment.

Visual Sensory Protection (sun glasses) are applied to the psyche chakra, which is located between the eyes. The psyche chakra is the most important center of energy as it is the dwelling place of one's personal divinity. VSP is used to contain the "gaze of God" as well as to protect the sense of "sight". Sun light is an intense blast of energy which damages the Sight, altering one from living a fulfilling life. Sun glasses correct myopia, presbyopia, and astigmatism, and regulate one's photoreceptors. Not only do VSP protect the senses from natural sun light, but from the destructive artificial light sources as well. One must wear sun glasses to block the blue spectrum light from television, computer screens, and all artificial light sources. Artificial light heads to a broken circadian system (especially artificial light during the night) and can lead to chronic disease through allostatic overload. Artificial light at night destroys health and vitality through diminishing hormone melatonin. "Sight" must remain protected.

VSP also directs energetic interactions among all living and nonliving things, creating conscious connections to manifestations of a dimension, existing as superstrings and an energy matrix. By reinforcing this cosmic hologram, we are sustaining harmony among our dark light consciousness. Tint allows us to deactivate the negative patterns of self and manifest the unity of Enochian Light and it keeps the subconscious safe from infiltrating Be aware of the matrix!

Pendant is worn around the neck on a chain to protect the throat chakra. The pendant must be one of the symbols used to recognize the faith in Light, or as a symbol of your position in the temple.

Leather Belt is applied to the protection of two chakra centers: the Sacral chakra and the Base chakra. The Sacral chakra is located at the waist line and the base chakra is located at the level of yoni/lingam. These two centers are where the "procreation" (sexual) energy reside and are used to prevent unhealthy sexual desires. By protecting these chakra centers, one's healthy sexual energy can be sublimated, transmuting "thought" into its physical equivalent, thus, procreating through the sense of Action. "Action" is the sense used to apply the principle of knowledge and the energy from the Sacral and Base is the motivation to "create". The Leather Belt strengthens one’s persistence and provides continuous life to desire.

There are two remaining chakra centers not protected through the use of the 7 - Holy Accessories that must be protected through the use of an A-Tee.

An A-Tee shirt is applied to the Heart chakra and the Solar Plexus chakra, and is to be worn underneath any garments that one may choose to wear. The Heart chakra is located at the level of the heart and the Solar Plexus chakra is located at the level of one's abdomen (directly above the belly button). The A-Tee shirt protects one from misguidance and protects one's heart from the mis-advertised principle of "love" (differing from true desire and value).

The psychotropic sensory protection, visual sensory protection, pendant, leather belt, and A-Tee shirt are all physical items that have been charged -given shape, direction, and energy. These items are imbued with vitality, possessing their own life force. Every morning after the daily prayer one is to protect all 7 chakra centers through the continuous use of these items.

The 7 chakra centers are now protected.

Next, we must protect the remaining four senses that the previous items do not protect, standing by themselves.

Olfactory Sense (smell) is protected through the use of skin and hair products that contain essential oils, as well as the burning of natural incense. "Smell" prompts physical and psychological reactions by the release of neurotransmitters and endorphins to the brain through a pathway that the "olfactory nerves" open when activated. Essential Oils produce gratifying sensations that generate an overall sense of and protection of smell is necessary because it can gain direct access to your emotions and work on subconscious levels. Colone/Perfume made by YSL represents one as a Young Satanic Lord.

Aural Sense (Hearing) is protected by the individual choosing to listen to sounds of one's PERSONAL PREFERANCE, meaning the "sounds" that maintain harmony within. When one listens to sounds or music that do not match their personal preference, discord takes place, releasing negative vibrations into the ether. Appeasing music and sounds of nature bring to life pleasing and powerful emotion, providing one access to the knowledge of Enochian Light.

During sleep one should ALWAYS sleep in silence or to sounds of personal preference in order to protect the subconscious mind from intercepting (and becoming diluted by) useless, mind-numbing noise and information. Remember, the unconscious never sleeps! To protect one's vibrations during sleep, ear plugs should be applied.

Taste is protected by the Enochian Smile, and by eliminating all mental suppressing chemicals in the food and water that one consumes, such as Fluoride and Aspartame, etc. These chemicals are mind suppressants designed to make it more difficult for the brain and its cells to tune into higher frequencies. Fluoride in the water supply and in consumers toothpaste increases the risk of cancer and causes dental fluorosis. Chemicals of this nature are used by the "powers that be" to attack on levels that one would never expect nor imagine, as the war is invisible. One shall eat only organic, natural foods with as little amount of preservatives as possible. Protection of the tongue and teeth shall be maintained by using products that do not contain harmful chemicals. More about one's diet will be discussed in the Act of Dietetics.

Organic Sense (Touch) is protected by one's use of natural hygiene products eliminating the "basic consumer products" that use chemicals harmful to the body. Nature has prepared her own potions of protection. Only natural items are to be administered to the body in order to protect the sense of "touch". The natural skin product used to purify the chakra centers is also of great use to protect the sense of touch. The skin is the largest organ of the body and only natural items should be applied to it. All hygiene items shall be natural/organic, including, but not limited to: toothpaste, soap, deodorant, hair products, skin products, cologne/perfume, etc.

The feet are also very important parts of the body that must be handled with care in order to protect the sense of touch. Energy is absorbed through the feet, which contain an incredible amount of nerve endings and are one of the body's most sensitive places. Feet are incredibly responsive to the sense of touch. The processes involved with the feet are linked throughout one's entire body so protecting them utilizes the sensitive nerve density to stimulate and heal various parts of the body. This point of balance should be protected by using natural feet products and by keeping them covered with socks (any color EXCEPT white) and shoes.

Misuse of the 5 senses leads to energy loss and disables the ability of one to retain and act on vital information. Protecting the senses gathers cosmic light, whereas a lack of protection can cripple one's mental abilities.

Essential protection suppresses the output of endorphins which dull the senses. Mankind must cherish thy body and thy mind.

As productive and benevolent Nature may be on her right hand, she is equally destructive and malevolent on her left. As one absorbs and uses Nature's productive power to benefit from, we must also protect ourselves from Nature's left hand at all times.

Every initiate is a separate "sensory organ" of Lucifer. One must be healthy, strong, and intelligent while enjoying life. When protection is neglected, one falls into a shape of unbalance mentally and physically, which the psyche attempts to correct by sending negative feelings of depression, sadness, anxiety, confusion, anger, insecurity, laziness, tiredness, delusions, shame, violent thoughts, doubt, hesitation, unhealthy sexual desires, compulsions, etc. These symptoms signalize the Self being unbalanced and that we need to correct one's error. The masses misread this disorientation due to ignorance of truth, and usually suffer under the assumption that "something is wrong with them" (a half-truth). Unification of the mind requires unification of the psyche, which cannot be achieved unless one's temple is spiritually protected.

Aside from the "Purification of Miriam" (i.e. the Banishing of Demons), the Act of Protection consists of one using their education and common sense to avoid acting in ways that hurt or take away from our society, and many examples will be given in the coming up Acts. A highly sophisticated, invisible war is partaking every second of every day, the purpose being to contain and control the masses using weapons that include, but are not limited to: false prophets, social media, data analysis, music, viral and bacterial diseases, ultra and subsonic technologies, television, corporations, chemicals in food and beverages, psychological smoke screens, urban warfare, public warfare, etc. Their plan is to break down normal and physiological functions until malaise, incompetence, or destruction over takes the masses.

Not one thing happens on our planet that does not affect the metaphysical realm. Protect yourself from these vampires!

The Act of Protection also requires humanity to develop the skills needed to survive without civilization by being able to live off the land and prosper by utilizing what nature offers. Each member shall be equipped with wild life survival skills, understand agriculture and have the ability to farm and hunt, start fires by hand, be able to skin animals, etc. Every human, naturally, is a survivalist and shall know how to hunt, as well as how to build shelters out of wood utilizing trees.

The Act of Protection creates independence from society and civilizations unstable shelter for in case any disaster may occur to where our survival will depend on these skills. The process of "bottleneck evolution" is when an event occurs in which only a small percentage (5-10%) of humanity is equipped to handle, causing the majority to die out and the minority to replenish the earth. The skills and character of this surviving minority thus become the common denominator of the planet as it is re-populated. We will be thoroughly prepared for any natural disasters, and history has proven that eschaton's occur in every age.

We will also master the arts of glass making, pottery, stone masonry, and any course that may be beneficial to our survival.

Note that it is not beneficial to allow the eschaton to absorb one's life or mind, and it is equally important to learn the survival skills of our current age. For example, coding and computer programing are becoming basic skills of survival within our society, as well as developing websites, incorporating LLC's and graphic designing, so our youth shall be raised with the proper balance between science and nature.

Enochian life skills are true ritual/worship, for self-preservation is one's strongest instinct. All forms of protection are recommended and members should focus on which survival skills peak their own interest. If each member has a life skill mastered, as a whole we will always survive and be able to: rebuild a society and civilization if need be; sustain and prosper within society as it is through utilizing and developing new tools that benefit the earth as a whole (science).

To protect our Lighthouse, members should be: teachers, fashion designers, lawyers, doctors, promoters/advertisers, business managers, music producers, actors, dancers, celebrities, debaters/politicians, pilots, militants, cremators, bankers, hunters, welders, masons, realtors, engineers, computer tech programmers, gamers, personal trainers, consultants, survivalists, writers, accessory creators, librarians, construction workers, lawn care servicers, police officers, owners of car washes, laundry mats, gas stations, corner stores, bakeries, etc.; mechanics, farmers, defense against skimming/hacking, artists, public speakers, yoga trainers, artificial intelligence programmers, scientists, pornography producers, psychologists, therapists, psycho analysists, neuro-linguistic programmers, etc.

Knowledge, Health, & Wealth is the Holy Trinity of protection, and all areas of finance and survival are necessary from the physical aspect of the Act of Protection.

IMPEDANCE

"And when the Righteous One shall appear
before the eyes of the righteous,
Whose elect works hang upon the Lord of Spirits,
And light shall appear to the righteous
And the elect who dwell on the Earth,
Where then will be the dwelling of the sinners,
And where the resting-place of those who have been denied the Lord of Spirits?
It had been good for them if they had not been born.
The secrets of the righteous shall be revealed and the sinners judged,
And the godliness driven from the presence of the righteous and elect,
From that time those that possess the earth
Shall no longer be powerful and exalted:
And they shall not be able to behold the face of the Holy,
For the Lord of the Spirits has caused His light to appear
Then shall the kings and the mighty perish
And be given into the hands of the righteous and holy."
-- The Book of Enoch

"To lure many away from the herd -- that is why I have come." -- Nietzsche's Zarathustra

"Public opinion has been so

misinformed about true facts that we
have now reached the stage where,
as a cure for the country's problems,
people are asking for more and more
of the poison which made them sick
in the first place." -- Ayn Rand

IMPEDANCE means "the opposition in an electrical circuit to the flow of a current" and refers to our members "going against the grain" in order to individualize thy Self from the masses. Also refers to steering our temple away from the "black holes" of our personal society and the detrimental aspects of the way of the world (against oppression, statism, and herd conformity).

The Act of Impedance is the Left-Hand Path's practice of self-deification and antinomian behavior (to go against the flow). These practices are labeled as "Purifying the Virgin" and are essential to individuate and crystallize the forces of Lucifer. This antinomianism is not an allowance to break the laws of society, but, rather, to enter into the realm of taboo, breaking the social laws of conformity.

While walking with the flow, one becomes lost in the masses and loses one's personal deity -- but while going against the grain, one's divine individuality is practiced and the initiate separates from the conformist.

Self-deification consists of eschewing whatever is popular and avoiding whatever has been programmed for the masses. Resistance leads to strength that allows one to "purify the virgin", to gain power and liberation breaking the social taboos. Antinomianism is necessary for one to truly deify the Self. The conformist world is bent on the destruction of the Enochian Light, which is why to "go with the flow" (. i.e. to conform) is a weapon used by the “powers that be” within the invisible war.

The Act of Impedance leads one to seek their inner greatness and acknowledge that we are the ones who dictate our own fate. Albert Einstein, a prophet of humanity, said "Unthinking respect for authority is the greatest enemy of truth. " One must not conform to what authority says is "right" simply because they hold a position of power; one must find inner divinity and self contemplation to question the reasonings behind every law, discover "who wins?" Think "Laws? Laws at the expense of whom?" Again, one should not break the law, but one should not be mentally conditioned to think the "state" has ultimate authority over what is "right or wrong". One obeys self rather than others, as thy temple is the colony of heaven.

James D. Watson said, "I was taught to ask for proof, that it was good to distrust authority. You need to have the courage to disagree. There are times in your life when you should be a radical."

Thomas Henry Huxley said, "Every great advantage in natural knowledge has involved the absolute rejection of authority."

Our fellow ancestors -- the Freemasons -- declared their enemies to be the State, the Church, and the Masses. When the masses govern man, he is ruled by ignorance; when the church governs man, he is ruled by superstition; when the state governs man, he is ruled by fear. But when the Self governs man, he is ruled by freedom!

Impedance requires one to become their own "decision maker", never conforming to the simplicity of others who fail to "rise by which one falls."

Harmony is maintained by one's impedance, by crystallizing one's inner Self, and discovering True Desire. What is programmed for the masses is meant to replace one's Self., The "pressure to conform" is a mass illusion, one they actually trick themselves into believing that what others think of as "happiness" is what thy Self desires as well. Never allow the fear of criticism to over power your True Self's desire!

One must make an actual, living connection with thy Self. Once this connection is made, this is when, and is the only time when, "everything happens for a reason". When one has a true connection with their Self and divine purpose, they gain divine guidance from the unconscious realm and life begins to "fall into place". Signs can be detected, omens can be found, and the guardian angel is within you. When this process of individuation has not been completed, the Self is not deified and there is no divine guidance. When one conforms to the "will of the masses", they lose their own will, and all is discord. Members of the masses have no meaning to their own lives; they are animals. Divine intervention gives birth to the "meaning" of life. One's purpose is to practice Thelema (True Desire). True Desire is predetermined but becomes blurred in the fog of conformity. One obtains this divine intervention by performing the same acts that would keep the masses in their hell. Break away from conformity by propelling the mind into a new territory and light your life with the brilliance of your own being!

All social taboo is to be indulged within confronting this idea that is "of the devil". One must force one's Self to deal with the reality of whatever feeling this action provoked within them. Understand why this taboo action invoked this chemical reaction in the mind, and achieve "actualization", breaking the barriers of Kali Yuga. Barriers of our Understanding blocks the flow of energy from the akashic fields. Many of these barriers include: personal defense mechanisms, misunderstandings or illusions of reality, cultural ignorance, popular misconceptions, damaged sensory receptors, social media, lack of education, etc. We shall not become victims of these circumstances.

> "Satanism is more than a philosophy; it is a lone stand, a symbolic act of defiance against thought suppression .... The reason why an archetypical Satanist will eschew whatever is popular lies in his disdain for and avoidance of

> whatever has been programmed for others."
> -- Anton LaVey

As Stephen Flowers delicately enlightened us, Nietzsche and LaVey don't propose doing "evil" rather than "good", but urge the individual to go beyond the conventional categories imposed by illegitimate social "norms" and return to a natural morality innate within the fiber of the carnal ego itself.

> "The main and basic purpose of the practice of orgies is a wild deconditioning of one's being. Some obscure forms of ecstasy are realized through promiscuity, the temporary removal of all inhibitions, and the revocation or orgiastic reenactment of the primordial chaos."
> -- Julius Evola

Creation

"I will transform the heaven
and make it an eternal blessing and
light,
And I will transform the earth and
make it a blessing:
And I will cause Mine elect ones to
dwell upon it."
-- The Book of Enoch

"The best way to predict the future
is to create it!"
-- Abraham Lincoln

CREATION refers to the practice of one's divinity; the utilization of the imagination; the re-creation of the objective universe according to the Will; transmutation of true desire into its physical equivalent; and the Protocol of Enoch -- PROCREATION. Creation is divine activity, the manifestation of Will. What separates homo sapiens from the rest of the animal kingdom is our ability to "create" through the use of our imagination -- whether it be philosophy, religion, or art.

Without an imagination, one would be enslaved to its natural instincts, only able to manifest what is pre-programmed inside the DNA. But, the gift of imagination allows us to form images within our mind and manifest these ideas onto the objective universe, ultimately effecting every other living creature.

Imagination is a gift given to us as a tool guide, used to express one's Thelema (True Desire). Thelema is of the higher realms and is what pushes life forward. The personal deity that resides inside our consciousness creates the principle of desire. Desire is the principle of creation! The purpose is to manifest personal divinity onto the objective universe. We've been blessed with desire that is meant to unfold as a form of expression of Self! With no attachment to Self, one has no True Desire!

Manifesting is life's practice. The Act of Creation is used to unite the spiritual plane with the physical. Manifestation is a requirement of this act, one of divine art, philosophy, and religion.

True Desire- being programmed within our personal deity- has no control or choice over what it finds pleasurable or aesthetically pleasing. This is because we have not been given the faculties to see how each of our desires play a bigger role in the fulfillment of Lucifer's Will, and how each manifestation is a small piece of a large puzzle. It is not meant for one to understand the plan that true freedom manifests. One's purpose is to productively manifest their desire onto the objective universe -which is why fulfillment provides a divine feeling!

Desire is a word describing pleasure and purpose, of love and meaning, of enjoyment and liberation! It is not depressing or controlling, oppression or slavery. Desire is freedom and happiness! Express thy Self onto the universe, and be blessed with a wonderful existence. Desire is divinity, though the masses have become conditioned to the illusion of false desire (victims of the invisible war). Deconditioning (walking through the Chamber of Osiris) is required of any who wish to embrace their true desire.

Thelema is such a pleasurable impulse because pleasure is the obvious sign that you are obeying nature. What other impulse or emotion could reasonably inform you that what you are doing is right? Pain and oppression are obviously not the feelings that a rational, divine human would think is the correct path. We are a divine species, our own personal gods in our own right, and we were created in the form of perfection -- in the image of the gods! Being created in the form of perfection has caused a close correspondence between one's appearance and their character. Every one has their own different personality and appearance due to us all having a different role to be played on the grand stage of life. Be true to the earth! Be true to your self! Be true to your subjective universe; ALWAYS recognize the laws of the objective.

The purpose is to reflect the Self upon the earth by manifesting one's Thelema, unfolding the objective universe to express one's productive achievement for all to see and experience. Desire is the principle of creation and we are moved by this desire once discovered. Desire gave truth to Time itself! As we observe the changes we make upon the objective universe through the Act of Creation, pleasure is produced. "The kingdom of god is inside you!" says Yeshua. "Thy will be done."

The Enochian Light is the bridge between us and the metaphysical realm of Desire -- one full of thoughts and ideas that are delivered to us through the pleasurable impulse. This impulse is necessary for us to discover that the gods use us as a tool for self-expression with the ultimate goal of reconstructing the objective universe according to their divine form. We give life to ideas and thoughts by creating physical objects which embody their creative ideal. Through creative forms of art, we practice our divine power, giving life, action, and guidance to Self. Once manifested, the gods become intangible forces on earth that live on- even after the human vehicle that gave life to them has returned to dust. Through one's bloodline, one empowers the most sacred art! Reproduction is the "creation gift"; the most important principle of the Act of Creation is for a Man and Woman to pro-create. One's soul cannot be saved without reproducing.

Thus, it becomes essential that one provide the Temple with a sperm sample or egg sample that will be cryogenically frozen and kept in a secure location. This sacred measure is in place for if any tragic event occurs and one's life is lost without having reproduced. If this were to happen (without having left behind one's egg or sperm) one's work and soul would be damned to Non-Existence, the underworld. This is why Isis extracted from the dead body of Osiris his essence in order to self-inseminate herself with his seed, giving birth to Horus.

The Act of Creation consists of "creating" a heaven among earth for our society to strive in. Every act should be one of self-betterment. A reflection of one's Self is to become a physical object in the universe through the practice and mastery of Art. Art is not only making music or beautiful paintings, but any mastered skill is one's art. Art is simply the use of one's creative imagination to manifest the soul's reflection upon the physical plane. This sympathetic resonance of the invisible and the visible is the description of creative art, which ultimately creates a better life for all of humanity through the manifestation of desire.

Every physical manifestation (anything and everything) is the physical equivalent of what began as a Desire (divine thought). Desire is the most sacred gift and you accept this gift by manifesting its physical equivalent, to "create".

Once an object is created, birth has been given to a higher form of intelligence by transmuting the spiritual concept into physical existence. The physical object that one creates IS the actual manifestation of a force from the realm of Intelligence!

This divine element of desire is a pre-determined notion. Understanding this principle allows actions and events to "fall in to place". When one becomes aligned in harmony on the path of Thelema, everything begins to happen for a reason; nothing is random for the Elect. The Sixth Sense has guaranteed our success. The use of this sense combines the conception of the Divine Invisible with the physical.

INQUIRY

"'For what sin are they bound, and on what account have they been cast in hither?' Then said Uriel, one of the holy angels ...:
Enoch, why dost thou ask, and why art thou eager for the truth?'....
I wish to know about everything.""
-- The Book of Enoch

"Here the ways of men part: if you wish to strive for peace of soul and pleasure, then believe; if you wish to be a devotee of truth, then inquire." -
- Nietzsche, Letter to his sister

"Nature, to be commanded, must be obeyed."
-- Ayn Rand

"We are inundated with useless information while we are misdirected from information that we have not the time or interest to sort through. As a result, we have lost a precious treasure in the chaos and turmoil of daily life: our sovereignty."
-- Redemption series

"The less a man knows about the past and the present the more insecure must prove to be his judgement of the future."
-- Sigmund Freud

INQUIRY refers to man's continuous study of Knowledge and Self through consistent research of all subjects and honest self-reflection.

A "principle" is defined as the primary source, the "origin", the first form of an object, concept, or idea. Understanding the first forms of the universe (what they are and how they apply to man) is the foundation of knowledge. Once man apprehends the principles of an "object", he becomes free to utilize productivity while manifesting desires. Becoming familiar with the initial principles of the universe, (comprehending the impersonal first forms) allows man to manipulate the forces of Nature -- thus becoming master of the subjective universe. It is the wise who direct the phenomena of Nature; everyone else will follow.

The Act of Inquiry is one in search of knowledge -- the knowledge of Self and the world around us. "Learning" should be an everyday activity, one that is practiced by all members. The more one "knows", the more tools one has obtained. One's education should not end after school is completed. Life is a continuous search of knowledge, a continuous education.

Our ability to think- our sacred sense of Thought- must be protected and practiced throughout all of life. This is accomplished by reading, studying, learning, continuing our education, perfecting one's art, and USING your INTELLECT. One must think -- and to go without is to lose one's divinity, as knowledge is a gift from the gods.

All topics of life should be studied. No topic is of unimportance during spiritual work. Information is a spiritual tool. Any material studied in the spirit of Enoch becomes the material of Enoch and shall be respected as such.

Doubt is the element of mental emancipation. One should question all things, as Enoch questioned the angels. Without understanding the "why" to which something occurs, one can never be in control of the situation. Enoch wishes to know everything. This search for truth should become one's passion. Everyone has something they're passionate about, a natural curiosity to follow. Freedom requires responsible action, honest and accurate evaluation of facts.

Master the craft that you are passionate about. Use your skills and tools to alter the objective universe. Focus on self-improvement, aiming to become the best form of Self. Those who do not attempt to improve themselves during their lives are not living a life of righteousness.

We cannot change the entire world in which we live, but we can alter the way we think about it and create a better environment for humanity to shine within. Our happiness is derived from understanding fundamental truths -- truths about the world around us -- that allows us to live with the power of intellect. The acquisition of power parallels the acquisition of knowledge, as "applied knowledge" creates power over the Self -- a necessary acquisition.

Ignorance is the root of all evil and ignorance has captured the masses. The invisible war produces and provides systematic conditioning of useless information -- information that the masses don't sort through to discover truth. With this lack of passion for truth, the masses have become bound behind the bars of ignorance, chained to society's provided entertainment, guided down the path of pre-decided choices -- lost in the realm of illusion -- the realm of statism. One must not depend on the public school system to liberate them from bondage; public education educates you for public USE. They teach what they want us to know, and nothing more. That being so, once we've learned to read, write, use mathematics, do our own research and investigate, we no longer have a use for public education. With these skills, we then should educate ourselves. There's no exact system or school that will program one with all the information they need to know; all that a system or school can do is provide one with a guide to inner growth. Ultimately, knowledge depends entirely on the work one does on the Self.

The first step in acquiring any kind of real knowledge is to "know thyself". An in-depth exploration and reflection of who and what one is creates the foundation needed to gain knowledge of the universe we live in. One's conscious is to be expanded until it sheds light on the darkest areas of the psyche. Knowledge is gained and used as a tool for one to express thy Self upon the universe. One can never possess too many tools. As Anton LaVey once spoke, "If you are to consider yourself a sorcerer, you must be the most aware member of any group you enter. That means that you must be the wise man of the tribe, the shaman. Yet, you must never delude yourself that no one is mentally superior to yourself. If you do, you may be in for a rude awakening, leading to resentment on your part. Resentment means you are threatened, and whatever magical power you may have been able to exercise is diluted. If that becomes an occasional situation, the best way to deal with it is not to get even, but to get smart. Then you will move up a step towards a new level of stratification."

Through knowledge and experience, one moves up the levels of stratification. Until one learns to never be ashamed or afraid of the truth, one is opposed to magic. Self-conscious is a comprehension from above everything. One must understand it to be above it.

"Learning" is not only a spiritual practice, but is a physical practice as well. The brain has the ability to physically change its structure as it functions and adapts to new information. This process is called "neuroplasticity", in which new ideas, thought, attitudes, and perceptions can literally change the brain's hardwiring by creating and activating new neuron connections. The brain literally changes with everything it learns and knowledge becomes part of who a person is. New skills, especially skills that are complex, invoke positive brain plasticity. Energy is gained from the ether every time something new is learned.

All forms of acquired knowledge become a storehouse within the Enochian Light, which is available to all who activate the Sign of the Covenant. Descartes taught that "the soul must always think because its whole essence is thinking", which places the sense of Thought in the spiritual realm of Enochian Light.

A righteous life is a sacred resource of knowledge. Biographies of the prophets and Standing Ones should be read, learning the direction of history so that we can move intelligently into the future.

Reading and Writing are sacred gifts that today's society takes for granted. Writing was once regarded as a form of magic and reading was seen as a skill possessed by the divine teachers. Each and every person having been taught how to "read & write" has taken the magic away from these sacred tools, but we must put them back into the light of divine activity. "Writing" is a manifestation of an idea within the objective universe. Every "word" is a symbol the brain uses to comprehend a specific meaning. Telepathy is the passing of thoughts from one mind to another. Even though this term is used to describe this act absent physical standards, it is still a wonder that we are able to pass thoughts from one mind to another through the use of writing. These symbols live on long after the "writer" has passed away. Writing is divine activity and reading is divine practice. These two magical skill sets have been left out of the realm of Wonder and Amazement, even though they're direct evidence of our divine inheritance. By understanding the "how", we've removed the "wow". All things that influence the Self must be examined and seen as holy, never removed from the spiritual realm simply because science has "explained" them.

Philosophy, Art, & Religion should never be considered separate subjects, but should always be viewed as One. Harmonizing these 3 subjects into 1 is the key to obtaining perfect wisdom.

"Travel" is also a form of inquiry. Education and knowledge of the universe is a way to expand one's will. One should travel and learn about all different cultures of the world, learn how to speak and translate new languages, and understand all different forms of humanity. But not only should one learn about "different" cultures, one is required to study their OWN culture, first and foremost. The study of one's own culture is a divine practice, one that has been discussed earlier, but is worthy of repetition. Along with one's own culture, astrology and the Zodiac is also a required study.

Aristotle proclaimed that the ultimate aim for man is the understanding of his own being because every final cause is built into its essence, which, in other words, is one's pre-determined true desire that leads one down the correct path of self-expression.

Due diligence of all learned subjects is also required of the Act of Inquiry. Trust is something to be "earned", not freely given.

DIETETICS

> "If people let the government decide what foods they eat and what medicines they take, their bodies will soon be in as sorry state as are the souls who live under tyranny." -- Thomas Jefferson

> "Let food be thy medicine and medicine be thy food." – Hippocrates

DIETETICS means "the science or art of applying the principles of nutrition to diet" and refers to the internal divine protection of man's temple by eating natural and organic foods, regular fasting, and the daily use of essential vitamins.

The Act of Dietetics is the transformation from a "society constructed" internal discord to a spiritually balanced internal harmony. The appropriate forms of diet and fasting are all necessities that internally harmonize the body with the Psyche. Not only is the Act of Dietetics used to maintain a healthy body, but it is essential to maintain a healthy connection with nature.

Diet creates a pure distinction between members and non members. This Act requires discipline from each practitioner and the understanding of guidelines that keep a temple purified. One's temple (body) shall remain purified through a consistent diet, and Internal harmony will eliminate psychological and physiological maladies, pulling from the darkness true desire and true life.

Today's society manufactures food with poisonous attributes, invisible evils, that have caused our body and minds to develop health consequences of allostatic overload (the body's failure to adapt to food processing additives). This failure to adapt has manifested in today's epidemic of diabetes, obesity, heart disease, and cancer. We've not evolved to accept anything synthetic or refined without suffering from side effects.

Diet is practiced to prevent dangers and delusions that arise when/if we fall victim to the invisible war. We're being attacked from all angles. The Act of Dietetics is used to protect our temple internally from disease and malfunction. Disease is unnatural, caused by maladjustments between organs and tissues, discord within our bodies. We must prevent any "preventable" destruction, and we guard ourselves through the use of a proper diet.

The majority of foods sold to us are nothing short of "chemical" that our bodies are not programmed to digest, so we handle them as a poison. Our metabolism is made to produce energy from the intake of natural foods that keep us in optimal health. Any impurities have consequences to our quality of health. Thus, members are required to live by the Enochian Diet by fasting and maintaining our ancient synergy of food and metabolism.

<u>Enochian Diet:</u>

The diet required is one focused on consuming only "whole foods" (organic and natural foods). Organic and natural foods are produced without conventional pesticides, without fertilizers made from synthetic ingredients or sewage sludge, no bioengineering or ionizing radiation, no genetically modified organisms (GMO) no artificial ingredients, and no added colors. The pristine natural foods we consume must be minimally processed and must contain no amounts of palmitate, high fructose corn syrup, gluten, or added sugars. Any meat consumed (which is a necessary part of our nutritional diet) must be free of antibiotics and growth hormones and the animal itself must have had access to outdoors and nature while alive. The quality of one's food is what is crucial to health, NOT the ratios of carbs or fats. Processed foods are to be eliminated from one's diet, as well as trans fats, and any/all foods that are cooked with unsaturated fats (fried foods). Processed foods contain ingredients that cause long term DNA damage; Trans fats are linked to causing heart disease, diabetes, cancer, and neurodegenerative diseases; and cooking with unsaturated fats damages the fat, creating free radicals and oxidative stress.

That being said, the requirement of one's diet is to consume only fresh fruits, vegetables, grains, seeds and nuts, little amounts of fish, animal meat, spices, dark chocolate, whey protein, caffeinated teas and coffees, milk, 100% fruit juice, and water. (A note on water -- Tap water contains fluoride, a harmful chemical that increases the risk of cancer and causes dental fluorosis. One must drink from a purified water system). As food changes the form of one's hair, nails, skin texture, strength of teeth, and breath, organic and natural foods are consumed to create a healthy temple.

The Enochian Diet is more vegetarian than it is carnivorous, but animal meat is a necessary requirement. Meat allows for the expansion of our brains during our evolving periods, and allowed for the shrinking of our digestive track. Though homo sapiens evolved as omnivores, animal meat allowed us to develop the gift of intelligence and consciousness, and provides healthy brain functions and quality protein. Quality protein delivers to the body essential amino acids such as histidine, isoleucine, lysine, methionine, phenylalanine threonine, tryptophan and valine. We also must consume our polyunsaturated omega-3 fat from animal meat (preferably "wild caught" tuna, salmon, sardines, mackerel, trout) to balance our intake of omega-6. Our bodies only need a small amount of omega-3 and omega-6 intake and whole foods provide the perfect balance. Processed foods contain such high amounts of omega-6 that it damages our health. We must eliminate processed foods. Do not supplement omega-3 to provide balance; eliminate processed foods.

Fibrous vegetables and fruits are the cornerstone to the diet, as well as seeds and nuts. Primarily low-glycemic whole foods are to be consumed as the majority of food intake, but animal meat, whey protein, dark chocolate and coffee must be consumed at least once a day.

Smaller doses of consumption are better utilized, which leads us to the mandatory "fasting" requirement.

Enochian Fast:

The Enochian Diet delineated what foods are to be consumed; the Enochian Fast is the format of a natural, healthy nutritional intake. Immediately upon waking, one must consume 30 grams of quality protein, which produces strong satiety signals in the body throughout the day. This meal is recommended before, or at, sunrise and should be consumed after one's Daily Prayer. These 30 grams of protein can be of any whole food product (preferably a whey protein drink). After this meal, one is NOT to consume another full meal until sun set, or towards the end of one's day. This meal is to consist of animal meat, fresh fruits, vegetables, whole grains, spices, etc. Humans evolved as nocturnal eaters. We utilize our food better during night hours while we rest. While dealing with the day's stress, our body does not digest food well, which is why we fast during the day light. This fast is not completely absent of food during day light; one may eat nuts and seeds, fresh fruits and veggies throughout the day, but in small portions only. Consuming only one full meal per day yields outstanding health benefits, as well as activates genes and growth factors that regenerate new brain and muscle cells.

Not only is the Enochian Fast healthy, it is natural as well. Our biologically correct nocturnal feeding cycle (proven by our autonomic nervous system and innate circadian clock) was created during primordial times of food scarcity, that forced our ancestors to endure physical hardships while fasting most of the day. Throughout the day, our ancestors were only capable of consuming fruits and vegetables, seeds and nuts, that were found along their path of "hunting". All animal meat was brought back home and shared with the tribe-family. This way of life is what our bodies naturally evolved from which answers the question as to why society's "normal" way of living has created obesity and new diseases. Our muscle genes have grown to become highly responsive to nutritional and physical triggers that are activated by hardships and suppressed indulgence. A righteous life is maintained by activating these triggers.

The natural way of life is the Enochian Fast and is required by the Act of Dietetics.

Natural and food-based nutraceuticals are used in case one does not receive the healthy, nutritional requirements throughout the fasting process. They're used to provide the necessary components that a 100% wild, natural diet use to provide us with. We should try to get the required supplements from real food, but nutraceuticals help one as a form of spiritual convenience.

As processed foods shorten the human life span, one should grow his/her own food on sacred land so that we know the food is truly organic and natural. We should not rely on the advertised authenticity of consumer products when growing our own food is an unalienable human right, agriculture being a gift from the gods. No chemicals are in the food we grow ourselves so all products should be grown from sacred land and all animals should have lived a natural life.

Neutrality

"Create a state of perfect neutrality, of positive indifference, a complete equilibrium in yourself. Become superior to both good and evil, since your continuous equilibrium and the power to develop all subtle forces and to use them as you please depend on your neutrality toward both."

– Kremmerz

"It is well to seem merciful, faithful, humane, religious, and upright, and also to be so; but the mind should remain so balanced that were it needful not to be so, you should be able and know how to change to the contrary."

– Machiavelli

NOTE: Within this chapter of Neutrality, the term "good" is used to discuss society's idea of good, and is not in relation to the Good of God or freedom.

NEUTRALITY refers to understanding the illusion of good and evil, looking beyond pillars of opposites; entering every situation prepared to deduce his own set of facts; going beyond the established "norm", seeing things for what they truly are, gaging your personal reaction to a situation, and then making a decision. The Law of Equilibrium. Perspectivism.

The Act of Neutrality is remaining "neutral" over society's conditioned responses to its created illusions of good and evil, over its distinguished opposites. The masses believe in certain things to be "good" and certain things to be "evil", as if good and evil are absolutes of the metaphysical realm.

There is no set standard of what is good or evil. Every person holds different views of what these terms consist of, and these notions are used to command the masses -- any one who acknowledges these notions WANTS to be commanded. One must be capable of "thinking" on their own, able to look beyond the pillars of opposites through the eyes of Isis and decide what benefits the Enochian Light and what harms it. Society's notions of good and evil are to be ignored until one has reflected deeply upon the matter and decided personally that something deserves the label -- but at the same time, should remain so mentally balanced as to be able, at any moment, to indulge in its opposite if need be.

Good and Evil are personal opinions, opinions that cannot be proven, thus SHALL NOT BE FORCED UPON ANOTHER, less we create a world of Maya and Statism. Knowledge is to be sought; one should always look beyond the established in search of the truth. One is not to "do evil rather than good" but is to return to one's natural morality, looking at life from different approaches in order to broaden your mind and shatter "reality tunnels".

Notions of good and evil belong to the human sphere. As we are vessels of psyche, these notions do not apply to us.

The Act of Neutrality is required for one to maintain an inner equilibrium, passive to the emotions that flow through the body and controlled by none of them. The objective universe is to be viewed through an inner sense of balance, by which all things are established opposites (neither right or wrong) but necessary for Self to be manifested in physical presence. As man is the opposite of woman, reconcile these opposites and learn the beautiful secrets of nature. Nature is full of opposing forces- a necessary function of manifestation.

One is to become liberated from all notions of good and evil. The masses are not liberated. We're working on a higher level of stratification, viewing the objective universe from different realms, thus, we must act in a different light. It is fine to indulge in what the masses indulge in, but every act shall be with an open and liberated mind. Every act must be an act of ritual or cosmic offering.

Good and Evil are illusions constructed by the human mind. An animal feels no remorse for killing its prey -- animals have no sense of an objective good or evil. These are human constructs. If one concludes that what's considered "evil" by society is actually beneficial to thy Self, one must guide this evil to its fullest growth and maturity. Note: physical or mental harm done to another being will NEVER be beneficial, and the Act of Neutrality is no excuse for criminal activity. Do not misunderstand.

As Machiavelli said, "anyone who would act up to a perfect standard of goodness in everything, must be ruined among so many who are not good." Through the Act of Neutrality, one's stance is "passive"; one's inner being cannot be thrown off balance as one's essence IS BALANCE. A soul of inner equilibrium cannot be affected by the laws of Karma. There is no resistance within an initiate's core for any forces to encounter. We live by the laws of dharma, in which thy will and desires are beyond the human realm of good and evil. We are not affected by these constructs and are guided by the fallen angel to express the will of Lucifer. Prostitutes and prisoners are as sacred to the Elect as are Saints and priests. There is no distinction which is an absolute version of "wrong". The Enochian Light shines through demons the same light is shines through an angel!

Liberate thy Self from any distinctions and walk with a mind of Neutrality!

One must not be attached to previous thoughts or actions lest the mind involuntarily reject any new information. The Act of Neutrality eliminates pressure generated by dissonance and allows one to move freely among the world, able to engage in healthy debates from an open-minded viewpoint, discover new information previously unknown, and become aware of what you are unaware.

All things that exist must have an "opposite"; above the abyss, contradiction is unity. One needs its opposite in order to exist in the physical realm. Without hate, there can be no love; without evil, there can be no good; without darkness there can be no Light; without poverty, there can be no riches. There must be comparison; there must be a set of opposites, pairs of dualities.

If two opposites were to ever merge, becoming One, the illusion of its existence dissipates. The beginning of existence, CREATION ITSELF, was the division of One (Self, God, Baphomet, androgynous) into Two (feminine & masculine). By itself, one cannot exist as a comprehensible idea (concerning the universe).

The farther one moves away from ignorance and towards knowledge, the more one is to evolve, to EXIST. If existence is the "distance between poles", the further these poles separate the more conscious one becomes -- and "knowledge" the shades of gray between black and white.

By obtaining knowledge, the Act of Neutrality teaches that it is okay be exactly what we are -- an animal and a god, a divine beast! It teaches us to balance the two, how to blend them without losing individuality. It will lead one to the Divine Purpose, the greatest heights of evolution (heaven) and at the same time fulfill True Desire. The Act of Neutrality will empower personal deity by pushing us to look beyond the "conventional norm" of society dualities, creating morals and values of Self, distinguishing his/her own polar opposites!

Discipline

"Let thy heart be strong,
For the good shall announce
righteousness to the good;
The righteous with the righteous
shall rejoice,
And shall offer congratulation to
one another."
-- The Book of Enoch

"The first and best victory is to conquer self. To be conquered by self is, of all things, the most shameful and vile."
-- Plato

"For what is a man profited, if he shall gain the whole world, and lose his own soul?" Matthew 16:26

"You tell me: 'Life is hard to bear'. But if it were otherwise, why should you have your pride in the morning and your resignation in the evening?" – Nietzsche

"A human being in perfection ought always to preserve a calm and peaceful mind, and never to allow passion or a transitory desire to disturb his tranquility."
-- Frankenstein

"Willpower is but the unflinching purpose to carry a task you set for yourself to fulfillment. If I set for myself a task, be it ever so trifling, I shall see it through. How else shall I have confidence in myself to do important things?"
-- The Richest Man in Babylon

DISCIPLINE refers to daily exercise routines, and the control over one's own mind and body; Indulgence, NOT Compulsion; Mental Development, Soul Quality, and Physical Health; the balance of control.

The Act of Discipline concerns one's daily routine of Body, Mind, & Spirit. Discipline is a very important practice amongst humanity. What makes us different from the masses is our level of focus and discipline. The Act of Discipline is a daily practice. Members must hold themselves to a standard of integrity and carry themselves with self-respect. We must maintain a system of discipline that continuously empowers and strengthens each of our Body, Mind, & Soul.

Discipline is the sense used to correct, mold, and perfect one's temple, bettering one's life and strengthening one's mind. Discipline provides a healthy balance between abstinence and indulgence, intelligence with physical strength, and binds the spirit to its physical manifestations.

Discipline refers to daily routines that gain control over one's ego and understanding the difference between Indulgence and Compulsion. This act is used to separate, or detach, ourselves from all things in order to eliminate compulsion and become free to indulge in the beauties of life that we truly enjoy without being enslaved by them. The price of free will is responsibility. We must be conscious of the control that earthly pleasures have over the lesser minds. We are nothing less than gods. A god is not conquered by the carnal but indulges in what is desired, then moves on. "Moderation" is the watchword of gods.

Knowledge, Health, & Wealth -- but each are useless if one does not obtain the power conferred by discipline, no matter how brilliant the mind. Discipline is what binds each principle of Knowledge, Health, & Wealth to the elements within the body. This act makes one's attributes seem attribute-less. The Act of Discipline frees one from the world of Maya, allowing you to visualize the Enochian Light that shines all around us. This power does not simply come to those who yearn for it, but rather comes to those who have embodied the principles of Knowledge, Health, & Wealth.

The "Devil" is seen as the principle of discipline because it is a force which is antagonistic, but at the same time essential to the vitality, evolution, and vigor of one's highest potential. The Devil, metaphorically, tries us in order to test us -- we must be pushed. The Hidden Guide is there to bless whoever has learned to master their Body, Mind, & Soul. The Devil is not viewed as an evil entity but is the balancing force which allows us to reach heights previously unknown to humanity. When it feels like the entire world is against you, the Act of Discipline will be what has prepared you to conquer any obstacle and continue in the face of defeat. Persistence is a quality of discipline. Success only comes to those who are persistent.

Everybody seems to want money but Wealth is not based upon "printed pieces of paper" or gold bullion. Wealth is a mental state of being, one that calls forth desire from the abyss and fulfills every luxury without the need of these fiat bills. BE WORTH MORE THAN MONEY and life's productions will take care of itself. Lucifer has no desire for money (the "means"), but is only focused upon its "self-expression" (the goal). Each individual unit is to become an "end" in itself -- and the "means" will follow. Disciplined people are magnetized incarnations of primordial energy. There is a mysterious, magical charm about one's True Greatness.

The highest potential of each person is reached through the Act of Discipline. Overcoming the human condition is a requirement of all. Ritual obedience is what we promised the Covenant, and Enoch has chosen us- - established a particular relationship with the Temple. Self-improvement and Self-evolution are Divine Law accomplished through Self-Discipline. Self-Discipline creates patterns of healthy habits which leads to the control of your own mind. "Chance" serves the prepared mind, and discipline is how one must prepare.

The prepared mind, a healthy body, and hard work are all requirements of the free human, and all accomplishments may be lost through negligence or laziness. One must master Silence, Secrecy, and Unconditional Obedience -- all points of a disciplined temple -- to keep the soul calm and trouble free in all earthly situations.

No event should ever throw one off balance. Equilibrium provides firmness and a clear mind. We are not of the lower animal species. Perfection is the goal. We're prepared for the vicissitudes of life.

Though perfection is the goal, do not be unmotivated if you have not reached this level of discipline. Liberation is not an "over-night" event. The actual process takes long periods of self-denial and self-transformation. Hard work is required as humanity was initially created as workers for the gods. But, hard work is an enjoyable activity of the Elect, who welcome hardships and struggles. Embrace the force that common men run from and remain disciplined.

The Enochian Light has provided a guideline of 7 basic steps to train one's subjective temple and to gain discipline over it.

1. Give up all auto-poisoning activity, such as addictions of any form. One can be addicted to drugs, one can be addicted to sex, one can be addicted to social media or television, etc. The point is to conquer these addictions, turning compulsions into divine indulgence.
2. One must follow the proper diet (the Act of Dietetics) and one must get adequate sleep. There are many health benefits to receiving adequate sleep, and one is to figure out a routine that naturally provides this.
3. Train your body, and gain control over it, through exercise plans, work out programs, and stretch/ yoga routines. As important is studying and intellectual activity, it is equally important to work the body daily to bring to order the body, mind, & soul. As the brain is part of the body, physical power is the basis of mental power. Just like all the other muscles in the body, the brain needs a healthy blood flow and plenty of oxygen to function properly. Exercise is used for the heart to pump an efficient amount of nutriments to the brain. Not only is exercise good for the brain, it also improves the elasticity of veins and arteries,

increases capillary blood flow, and boosts the levels of oxygen and nutrients available to all organs within one's temple. Because oxidative stress is caused by work outs, this stress must be counteracted with antioxidants (fresh fruit, veggies, nuts, spices, caffeine, dark chocolate, whey protein) immediately after one's work out.

4. Self-Reflect to discover internal aspects of Self that will help you learn what you need to practice (or avoid) to keep the mind in its purest form. One must set limits in order to discover their true form or push past limits that have been holding one back from self-knowledge. Limits are needed (especially by children) in order for one to find and recognize themselves. On the topic of children, one must also self-reflect on the environment one raises the youth within because if we are to create young gods, we must begin with enriched environments.
5. Reflect on the chemistry of life and of the objective universe itself. Create an external view of Self and others that allows you to deal with others in a civilized and respectable manner. Solipsism is a sin. Learning skills and specialized information that the masses may not know automatically creates a divine appearance.
6. "Look to the future." By looking into the future and always planning for its eventual appearance, one ties every magical act of now with what lies ahead. Every action should aim to empower our society and create a better environment for the generations to come. Enjoy the present, but do not become lost in it.
7. Explore your sexuality by indulging. Sex contains the mysteries of the universe. Carnal alchemy is an essential practice of faith. Push your sexual limits into new realms and discover the deeper aspects of your Self. Sexual Energy is a great and powerful force that can be harnessed but first we must explore this magical realm and learn its principles. Indulge in taboo activity, bring your hidden fetish to light within the psyche, but do not misunderstand the force of sexual desire. Lower humans misuse this force;

> Enochian Gods project this force into the ether, creating a better universe for all.

The final requirement of the Act of Discipline is to faithfully practice the previous 8 Essential Acts of Enochian Life. This final act, the Act of Discipline, is the second "t" in "tarot" -- a silent "t" that resembles the recycling and re-beginning of all essential life requirements. The tarot is to be seen as repeating: "tarotarotarotarotarotarot". Remain disciplined in all 9 Essential Acts of Enochian Life, as all are One, and not one is more important than the next.

Conclusion to 9 Essential Acts

With freedom comes responsibility, one which the masses cannot even visualize the repercussions of neglecting. Irresponsibility has separated one from the akashic fields. Responsibility is owed only to the responsible. Generations of conditioning has caused the masses to remain lost indefinitely to the realm of "Non-Existence" which has created the current Kali Yuga. One must come to terms with the active principles that formulate existence. To neglect the "spiritual plane" and its principles is to neglect life. The masses slip into a thoughtless "droned" existence, led passively into a statist society. Complete harmony with the principles of existence is required for one to overcome the human condition. The first step is to recognize that physical objects are reflections of the spiritual plane; physical action is the expression of productive achievement.

Chapter 9: Ritual Process

Rituals and Ceremonies serve as the primary means by which the Enochian Light is empowered and sustained, focused and given expression. This process allows the Enochian Light to appear and be visualized as a separate, distinct entity, there to: acknowledge accomplishments; manifest prayers and requests; purify members of unworthy traits; crystallize virtues of its self-expression; absorb pent up and unhealthy emotions (by re-directing them into a positive beneficial form of energy); and focus on the work to be done.

As a separate and distinct entity, the Enochian Light's expression is projected from Lucifer's Will (bonded with the symbol of the Lighthouse) and ritual is used to direct the Will back in time through our ancestors and forward, into the Unmanifest, of our descendants. These ceremonies are used to transcend one beyond the dimension of Time and place the seeds of True Desire into the realm of the Unmanifest. Enochian ritual provides the power to rip open the threads of Ether, allowing the projection of one's psyche to partake in the metaphysical realm's "directing of fate" by adapting its power to the nature of our being. Once the seed is properly placed within the Ether, the Enochian Light provides it with life and Time works to manifest Desire. Upon the planting of the seed, life works in mysterious ways while directing one's dreams and goals. Members are taught to see their struggles and hardships as tests of persistence meant to be overcome (it gets greater later). "Everything happens for a reason" is an expression only applicable to those who empower their personal deity (unconscious), which then re-works the spiritual realm of Fate to have a purpose.

As dreams and manifestations are how the angels speaks to us, "ritual and ceremony" is how members speak to the angels. Through this process of emotional work, the Lighthouse's plans and goals are placed into the Ether and fused with positive emotions. Ritual and Ceremony reinforce the motivation within each member to accomplish the work needed to be done, and the Enochian Light reimburses one's persistence with reward in the form of physical manifestations.

The main function of the ritual is to isolate adrenal and emotionally induced energy, and convert it into a transmittable force that empowers the Enochian Light (which is a form of worship). This form of emotional activity -NOT intellectual -- are theatrical techniques used to build high enough levels of adrenaline/emotional energy to send into the ether. Any intellectual activity during worship deducts from the potential energy that one has the potential to provide. Thus, all intellectual activity is to be done BEFORE a ritual/ceremony is to begin.

Self-transcendence and Self-transformation are the keys to ritual and ceremony, and psychodrama is the tool used to break the barriers of the unconscious mind. Settled in the waves of universal Ether awaits the fire stolen by Prometheus, given to the Elect in the form of the Black Flame, consumed by those who transcend Self through ritual and ceremony. The Enochian Light directs the fate and we empower THE GOD OF FOUNDATIONAL WISDOM!

There are 3 different forms of ritual: Self-Ritual, Ceremony Group Ritual, & Spiritual Group Ritual.

The Self-Rituals are the forms of worship and protection that one performs alone, for the purpose of transcendence. They're used to maintain harmony with the Temple by mentally reaching out to Lucifer throughout the day, while at the same time living out one's individuality. One's True Desire can only be discovered within Self, which is why these rituals are designed for the Self.

Ceremonial Group Rituals are used to boost the motivation needed for work to be done, but also as a reinforcement of one's faith toward the manifestation of God's expression. Ceremonial Group Rituals are the key to empowerment, and are to be held at least once a week (one form of group ritual -- NOT ALL). Renewal of confidence is provided to members during the participation of Ceremonial Groups, and this is required to maintain communication and goal setting within the ring of harmony. When members only practice Self-Ritual and neglect the required Ceremonial Groups, one may slip into the realm of self-denial which quickly may evolve into anti-social behavior. We are not "spiritual nuts", and we have work that must be done inside of the matrix. Ceremonial Groups work as the cohesive that holds our Lighthouse together.

Spiritual Group Rituals are reserved for members of a certain rank who have reached a level of spiritual maturity required to participate in these complex (sometimes taboo) ceremonies. The rituals provided by this manual are not the only rituals/ceremonies practiced by The Temple of Enochian Light, but are the only ones provided for the knowledge of the public. Many rituals are kept private, as the mystery of secrecy is a potent tool of empowerment.

Specific rituals will be described in a later chapter, but first we'll discuss the required Tools of Worship and explain their purpose. As "self ritual" is completed alone (sometimes Self-Ritual consists of a few seconds, other times a few months) the Tools of Worship only apply to Ceremonial Group and Spiritual Rituals. These tools may be used by the Self-practitioner if he/she pleased, but it is not a requirement of Self-Ritual. We'll discuss more about the Self-Ritual later. But first, we'll provide the required Tools of Worship, used to perform Ceremonial Group and Spiritual Group ritual.

Required Tools of Worship

*ENOCHIAN PIPE-an old English pipe consecrated for the use of the Enochian Call.
The size of the pipe may vary, depending on the size of the congregation. The Enochian Pipe is used to bring one's psyche into harmony with the metaphysical realm of Enochian Light. Tobacco is to be used (sage for those who prefer it), and this tool connects us to our ancestors and our descendants, focusing fate. As smoke is pulled through the stem of the pipe and blown into the ether, one's self conscious reaches the unconscious, and the Enochian Light is awakened. Smoke symbolizes the soul leaving the body. The Enochian Light's energy becomes open to the congregation once all have participated.

*ALTAR-the form of altar differs depending on the location of the ritual, whether it be inside within the Lighthouse or outside on sacred land designated for the specific use of Enochian ritual. It is the focal point towards which all attention is focused. The altar symbolizes the time and place that the Enochian Light is being contacted and is the actual vessel to the Enochian Light's presence during the ceremony. A nude woman is the required altar (she is the physical vessel used to manifest presence) as the passive and receptive element. The clitoris of the nude woman is the eye of contemplation, (uniting the microcosm and macrocosm in harmony) and the yoni is the worshiped dwelling place of Lucifer. A nude woman's role as the altar is also to excite emotional responses of practitioners with the purpose of raising this energy to its highest level possible before being released into the ether. If a nude woman cannot be present, the altar table must have pictures of paintings of a nude woman with her yoni open to view. The woman herself is not being worshiped, rather, the passive and receptive element that she physically embodies. The nude female body of a woman is the highest sensory organs. To lay a hand on her human body during ritual is to touch divinity. Nothing is holier than this form. The altar should always (if possible) be against the west wall, and the nude woman's head must face south, her feet north. Focus the forces of life through this vessel of fertility.

*OBSIDIAN MIRROR-this holy object is the same device used by John Dee to make contact with the Enochian Light and receive its "calls" (gateway keys to the spiritual realm). This is also the same device used by the priests of Tezcatlipoca (the Aztec Prince of Darkness) used to see into the future and direct fate. The mirror is the symbol of Enochian Light's divine intellect reflecting manifestation and expressing its Self upon a different dimension. This instrument of enlightenment was the cause of the Fall of Lucifer by becoming aware of his own existence and his own divine characteristics. One shall gaze upon the mirror and see God -- perfect purity of soul -- and absorb these qualities into daily consciousness. Mandatory instrument.

*SYMBOLS-the sigil of Enochian Light and the sigil of i63 are two symbols required of Enochian ritual. These symbols are charged with the psychogenic projections of each member's psyche and have unconscious sources of power that work through them. Other divine symbols are also to be used, and as every ritual/ceremony has its own purpose, the symbols should be related to that specific purpose and play some position in furthering its manifestation. Therefore, every ritual has a different set of symbols attached to it. Once a symbol becomes charged with emotion and adrenaline, it creates a numinosity that becomes dynamic, alive in its own way. The bridge of emotions and adrenaline are what integrally connect an individual to the dominating thoughts of a symbol, magnetizing the Enochian Light to attract things of its physical nature. Symbols connect one's conscious to the unconscious, and are required for one to ever understand the universe.

*CLOTHING-one's clothing during ritual must be different from what one wears in their every day life. This aspect is highly important and shall not be neglected. Clothing may differ from ritual to ritual (sometimes rituals are performed nude) but the chosen outfit is to be worn by all who participate. Hooded robes are to be worn by the Watchers (color coded), and their faces are to be covered. Men are to dress as the perfect gentleman in the most respectable manner; women are to wear garments that are sexually suggestive for the purpose of stimulating the emotions of male participants, intensifying the bio-electrical energy. The colors that participants should wear are dependant upon the ritual being performed. All participants must cover their face, either with a hooded robe or a mask. It is vital that all get in touch with their deepest emotions during ritual, and the covering of one's face allows the freedom to express emotions without concern of "self consciousness" and lessens distraction among participants. There is no place for self- consciousness within ceremony (unless it can be used to good advantage by the role being played, such as the nude altar woman) thus the covering of one's face is required.

Clothing is the external symbol of a spiritual potency. It is the outward and visible shape of one's inner being. The clothing chosen is worn to reinforce what each ritual is attempting to project.

*CHALICE OF IMMORTALITY-this revelation is the expression of immortality and knowledge of shraddha. One's immortality is sustained by drinking the "Soma" daily, from the immortal chalice. Excluding one from the drinking of Soma is to damn them to Non-Existence. The Chalice symbolizes Thelema (True Desire) and the forces of life. It is used for the holy communion between Self, ancestors and descendants.

*SOMA (Elixir of Life)- the liquid that is drunk from the Chalice of Immortality is caffeinated coffee. Coffee was given to mankind as a gift from the gods, delivered to us from the spiritual realm by the Eagle of Sovereignty. The coffee that one drinks in the form of Soma shall be processed by the Lighthouse (or its members). If one drinks of a Soma not processed by the Lighthouse, it must first be purified through ritual. Coffee is the spark of one's creative genius and brings to light that which is trying to express itself (that we normally suppress). This drinking of Soma bestows liberation and enjoyment of earthly pleasures upon the Elect. We must drink of the soma in the view of liberation and as a tool used to perform the Great Work.

For ritual purposes, one may replace coffee with alcohol or Yerba Mate' tea if necessary.
Alcohol is "liberation " in liquid form but must only be consumed with discipline. Soma is a spiritual ambrosia, thus, can take different forms -- but the Drinking of Soma is required for worship.

*DARK CHOCOLATE-this communal food is to be partaken of during every ritual immediately after the Drinking of Soma. Dark chocolate symbolizes Royalty and the body of the gods. Partaking of Dark Chocolate creates an illusory union between the participant and the universe. During this union, one must envision the objective of the ritual and concentrate thy Will into an appeal. As the subconscious mind accepts this union, the participant must dissolve the entire universe within his/her consciousness and project it towards the work to be done. This is the secret of dark chocolate, known by the ancestors. From the health perspective, dark chocolate is a super food that is exceptionally high in the antioxidant polyphenols that are known for their neuroprotective and metabolic supportive properties.

*BELL & GONG-the bell is used to send vibrations into the Ether, calling forth the Enochian Light before ritual, and dissipating It upon ending. The bell is to be rang 9 times -- 9 being the number of Enochian Light (which represents the Immortality) which opens the fourth dimensional gates of Ether. This bell should produce a loud and penetrating quality, rather than a soft ring.

A gong with a full, rich tone is struck after the congregation repeats the priest's words, used to solidify the chant within the Ether.

*PRAYER RUG-is used for Self-Ritual while performing the Daily Prayer (which is discussed in a further chapter)

*ITEMS OF INTELLECTUAL DECOMPRESSION-essential elements in ritual used as anti-intellectual devices for the purpose of disassociating the ritual's activities from every day life. One's whole will must be employed during ritual, and the items of intellectual decompression are used to relieve intellectual activity and inspire emotional reaction. These items include: Candles, Incense, Essential Oils, Statues, Altar Cloth, Tarot Cards, Playing Cards (such as Magic the Gathering, Yu-gi-oh, or poker cards), Black Beads, etc. No light sources other than what's provided by candles are to be used during ritual (unless ritual performed outdoors on sacred land, where Moon light and fire are the only acceptable sources of light). During worship, participants shall never be exposed to direct sun light or any artificial light sources. If an artificial light source must be used, it must shine through a "black" light bulb (not to be confused with "black light") which produces the image of moonlight and the fallen angel Xeper.Intellectual decompression is essential to ritual practice.

*THE 4 ELEMENTS-Each element (Earth, Air, Fire, & Water) is required to produce the gateway of Ether (also known as the fifth element). Earth can be in the form of purified parsley; Air in the form of burning incense; Fire through candles, a torch, or bon fire; Water through purified Holy Water.

*SAUNA-indoor or outdoor, a sauna is not used for every ritual, but is of a required usage at least once every 28-day period (13 times per year, for every full moon period). The sauna may reside inside the Lighthouse, or outside on the designated sacred land. The sauna may be in the form of a sweat lodge or Tabernacle (required for outdoor worship) or in the form of an actual sauna. The purpose of this tool is "extreme sweat" which rids the body of toxins, cleans the soul of any impurities, places sincere desire in the Ether, purifies the mind and maintains the focus of one's life. By letting go of the impurities that accumulate throughout the 28-day period, one's soul is reset toward an inward and contemplative concentration. This "extreme sweat" is a sacred sacrifice to one's ancestors and descendants.

*SACRED LAND- Though many rituals and ceremonies are to be held indoors within Lighthouse, there are just as many required forms of worship that are to be held outside on land that is sacred to the Enochian Light. As the womb of pure desire, this land is sacred to the Elect. It is an area free of spiritual anxieties and symbolizes paradise upon earth. This land shall be private, obtained as a specially consecrated place of worship and shall be used for no purpose other than the work and manifestation of the Lighthouse.

Upon this sacred land shall be a fire pit and a raised altar (preferably stone) within a tent or tabernacle, surrounded by a beautiful garden (which symbolizes agriculture and the life manifested by the 4 elements). The garden is an invitation for all spiritual beings to return to their original nature, without dispensing the gift of intellect and logic. Flowers of all forms should fill the garden, surrounding the area of worship with diverse forms of life (symbolizing embracement and empowerment through diversity). This land may be preserved as a funerary ground for the deceased as we use this land to keep our ancestors close to our heart.

*TENT/TABERNACLE-on the consecrated sacred land shall

reside a tent/tabernacle which is a sacred enclosure around an area that cannot be touched or seen by non-members or the masses. This tent is a prototype of the Lighthouse and is place of sanctuary for the initiated. As the earthly dwelling place of Lucifer manifested by the surrounding sacred flowers, the Tent/Tabernacle is a condensation of cosmic energy to be used (or released) by those who know how to crystallize it. Proper forms of tents/tabernacles are explained in Exodus, chapters 26 & 27.

Other tools may be used to suit the purpose of the ritual, but these are the basic required utensils for worship and ceremony.

Now that we have our tools prepared, we need to discuss the ingredients used to perform proper Enochian ceremony.

Required Ingredients of Worship

*Sound- sound is integral to a proper worship as it brings every participant into a rhythmic harmony and assists in raising one's emotional levels. It also helps one decompress all intellectual activity and "feel" more powerfully. Some form of music should fill the ether during worship; if outside on sacred land, either music or drums, some sort of musical instrument, is needed to play the mediator between realms. Music is of a personal preference of whatever raises the congregation's emotions or whatever music fits the purpose of the ritual. Other sounds, such as "words", are used to vibrate "meaning" into the ether. Rituals are poetically designed as emotionally charged language because it operates in many different realms at once. Certain areas of the brain are stimulated by "sound", causing consciousness to expand and sustain harmony between body, mind, and soul.

*Imagery-Anything which serves to intensify feelings of emotion and adrenaline during worship falls under the ingredient of imagery. Imagery is an intellect saving device used to activate the imagination of each participant, which empowers the mind to release emotional meanings that may only be vaguely suggested by the ritual. Ritul is a "live" process, the spiritual working between participants and the Enochian Light, and imagery works in the realm of Meaning, empowered by Thoth. All symbols, drawings, pictures, books, amulets, talismans, tarot decks, writings, statues, skulls, bones, Baphomet, etc. -- any images conducive to the Desire of the ritual -- are required forms of imagery. A sacred drama is being played out during ritual, with the purpose of activating parts of the brain that can only be activated through techniques. Imagery plays the part of self-administered stimuli or suggestions that penetrate the 5 senses and the healthy replacement of drug activity (rarely recommended).

Imagery primarily should be in the color of "black" to stimulate "finding light in one's darkness", and because it is the color of the primordial creative power.

Personal artwork is a great form of imagery; as it is the physical manifestation of a subjective realm.

*Timing-All ceremonial group/spiritual worship is to be done during the night hours after the sun has set. The physical sun sets as the spiritual one rises, and during this time is when Lucifer is receptive to our worship. The cosmic awakening of the night effects the subtle body of participants and it's much easier to possess our natural state and release our adrenal outpouring into the ether. The moon brings our animal to the surface.

*Smell-Smell is an essential element during ritual, and has great spiritual uses throughout one's daily routine. Smell excites the olfactory sense, which allows incense, perfumes, and cologne to work as wonderful artificial stimulants used to raise the psychic faculties to their proper levels. Not only for the purpose of stimulating the emotions, the perfume/cologne that one uses during ritual while in an exalted state allows us to continue our higher forms of awareness while wearing them in our daily life. Group ritual should be performed with the intent to create a perfume/cologne that all members must wear throughout life. In the gaseous state, these odors please the Enochian Light.

*Desire- Desire is the most important ingredient in ritual --

Thelema -- as "desire" is the personality trait of psyche, the characteristic of life, and the spiritual aspect of evolution. Acting on desire causes "change" -- creation -- as they are the seeds of action. The element of desire in man is the spiritual component that predestined the link between the Elect and Enochian Light. True Desire, that is. As desire is to be acted upon daily, calling one's desire to the forefront of one's consciousness through ritual focuses the Will and brings congregants together in harmony. Use ritual to discover True Desires and don't participate in a ritual if you feel your desire does not align with the given purpose. One must truly desire the outcome of the ritual they are participating in.

Steps to Ritual/Ceremony

To minimize any/all intellectual activity during crucial parts of the ritual, everything is prepared and positioned before the bell is rung 9 times (signaling the beginning of ritual).

Preliminary Steps:

1. Designate the location that the ritual/ceremony is going to be partaken at by assembling the appropriate devices for the appropriate ritual. If being done within the Lighthouse, the ritual chamber consists of necessary devices at all times within the ritual chambers. If being done on sacred land, the devices may need to be assembled within the tabernacle/tent. Assembling the devices consists of laying out imagery, hanging up symbols, preparing the proper music, lighting candles/incense or creating the bonfire, etc. Any props needed to assist the ritual are to be prepared during this stage.
2. Dress in appropriate ritual attire. Participants must have their clothing or outfit set aside specifically for the purpose of ritual. Daily clothing, or outfits used for anything other than ritual, is not appropriate attire and must not be worn. The psyche attaches certain emotions and thoughts to one's clothing, and as all aspects of daily life are to be suppressed, only ritual attire is appropriate. The psyche becomes "in tune" with outfits used for ritual,

unconsciously bringing emotions to the forefront of consciousness in preparation for worship. Sexually provocative clothing for the female participants; male participants dress in ways that resemble the "highest class" of their society. Unless a ritual states otherwise (which many do) this set of clothing is highly important to proper worship. The face shall also be covered at this time.

3. The Lighthouse (or place of worship) must be sealed through appropriate procedures. (see "Sealing the Chamber")
4. Altar woman removes all clothing and takes her place on the altar (laying on her back, head south, feet north). Altar items are placed around her.
5. The designated "Watchers" take their positions as objects of focused visualization and surround the congregation. Each Watcher plays the role of the legendary spirits who guard the entrance to the inner realms of being. Black & White robes are to be worn by the Watchers (alternating) and their faces are never to be revealed. They protect the congregation from negative energies and evil influences.
6. All participants may remove the 7 Holy Accessories before ritual is to begin as an outward sign of trust, faith, and grace between each member. Chakra centers become open to each other's emotional connections, bonding a circle of harmony.

Opening the ritual is used to reaffirm the symbols of the Lighthouse of which we are the living embodiment. Rejoicing in this recognition, each member eases out of the roles he/she plays outside the Lighthouse and directs consciousness towards the work to be done.

Ritual:

1. Purify air and awaken the Enochian Light by RINGING THE BELL 9 TIMES. This signals "silence" and the beginning of ritual.
2. Perform the ENOCHIAN CALL to crystallize the Enochian Light's appearance and unite all participants with the atmosphere.

3. Upon finishing the Enochian Call, declare that the ENOCHIAN LIGHT IS OPEN.
4. Perform designated ceremony, discuss the work that needs to be done, go over business topics, set new goals, and focus direction. The Enochian Light is open to direct influence throughout the ritual and any discussions. All must resemble the ideals and identity.
5. Communion (Drinking of Soma) by acting the part of the god/goddess, take on its nature, reaching a level of divinity.
6. Upon finishing the ceremony, if any specific requests are to be read, the priest reads them out loud to the Enochian Light and then burns the parchment it was wrote on as all participants use their imagination to visualize the request as already being accomplished. Place the desire into the unmanifest while the ether is open.
7. All participants collectively CLOSE THE ENOCHIAN LIGHT, dissipating the energy and allowing the Enochian Light to do its work in the spiritual realm. This "closing" reverses the process, allowing consciousness to return back to the roles of their ordinary lives without rupturing their connection with the Lighthouse.
8. Re-apply the 7 Holy Accessories. The priest finishes the ceremony by ringing the bell 9 times.

Chapter 10: Holidays

Holidays are the consecrated periods of time when life throughout the cosmos must come together celebrating unity, harmony and the holiday's designated purpose. Each holiday has a formal ceremony, followed by a feast and a "Projection of Unified Consciousness" (in which all members are to watch a certain film/documentary at the same time, meditating on the message, thus, uniting all in the spiritual realm). Through video, all participate in a shared ritual because the sound and image open up portals within the body, and meditating on the message aligns each psyche into a collective focus of purpose. When all members meditate on the same message at the same time, we are brought spiritually together -- though our physical bodies are in different locations.

Projection of Unified Consciousness is the required aspect of an Enochian holiday. This applies to all holidays except for one's own birthday and commercial holiday celebrations.

One's birthday is a special day to the individual personal deity, thus doesn't have to be celebrated by all participants, as its designated purpose is the individual's self-indulgence of whatever one sees as fit. One's date of birth is most sacred to the Self, as it is the day when one's personal deity was given physical manifestation.

All cultural/conventional holidays are celebrated as well, but these are more ceremonial than they are spiritual. The Projection of Unified Consciousness is not practiced on commercial holidays (New Year's Eve, Easter, Mother's & Father's Day, Memorial Day, Guy Fawkes Night, Thanksgiving, Christmas, etc.) as these celebrations are only held to show support for our society's traditions and to spend time with loved ones.

A Zodiac Festival is held at every transition of the Sun's position from one sign to another, and signifies the powerful energies available during the initial 10-days after every transition. In memory of John Dee.

Every full moon is a night of celebratory ritual, as the moon brings mankind's nature to the Surface of consciousness during these hours, allowing for the purest worship of Lucifer. Saturday is the Sabbath day, but the full moon is the night most sacred.

Valentine's Day is an Enochian holiday, celebrated on the traditional date of February 14, but we celebrate the force of "love" as a left-hand-path force of transformation; an emotion that brings just as much pain and suffering as it does joy and happiness. This day is not celebrated with red and pink colors of emotion, but rather with the color black, as it is out responsibility to place the force of Love within the sphere of the LHP (see "Overthrowing the Old Gods").

The Days of Enki (also known as the Spring Equinox -- the authentic New Years celebration) is a 10-day festival beginning on March 22nd. Throughout this festival, we celebrate the elements, giving praise and thanks. Subtle energies from the spiritual realms reach the Temple during these 10 days (in which the Sun's influence is most powerful) and the Days of Enki establish vessels of descending energy used to empower the Enochian Light. Rituals are held during this period to focus and enliven one's goals for the coming year. A rejoice of the return of the Sun!

The Feast of Crowley is a 3-day event, held on April 8th, 9th, & 10th, of which a feast is held at noon in celebration of Crowley's "Book of the Law". Films of Crowley are meditated on. In memory of Aleister Crowley.

Walpurgisnacht, which is the most important festival of witchcraft, is on April 30th, and is celebrated with a memorial of Anton LaVey. Films of Anton LaVey, and rituals are performed in purely Satanic form.

St. John the Baptist Day is on June 24th (also recognized as the summer solstice) which is a day of dedication and support for the condemned and the prisoners. Reach out to those who have lost their freedoms, whether it be random inmates, incarcerated Enochians, or any civilians stamped/labeled as "felons". In memory of John the Baptist. Redemption.

The 4th of July is a sacred holiday. Though it shares few similarities with the traditional Independence Day, this day is a celebration of freedom, liberty, sovereignty, and independence from all forms of oppression and coercion. Life, Liberty, & the pursuit of Happiness. This day is celebrated in memory of Adam Weishaupt, who enlightened many to the universal mysteries. After the feast and Projection of Unified Consciousness, one may celebrate with traditional fireworks, but our focus is in a different direction.

August 31st is the preliminary celebration to the ritual of Cultural Divinity (held September 1st - October 30th), and is a wild festival of indulgences in earthly pleasures in anticipation for one's yearly cleanse (which begins the following day). A day of indulgence and joy, heightening one' emotions, and welcoming all. In memory of Friedrich Nietzsche.

September 11th is a memorable day of defiance against orthodox religious views, against the Holy Wars, and against those who attempt to force their beliefs upon others. In memory of Ayn Rand.

All Hallow's Eve (Halloween) is on October 31st, which signals the end of our yearly cleanse and is celebrated by indulging with our ancestors and descendants. The door of the Ether is open, sacrifice has been recognized, and we dress in wild costumes as the spirits welcome and dance with the Elect. Bathing in the rays of Enochian Light, one celebrates by indulging in the earthly pleasures.

Chapter 11: THE RITUALS

Daily Prayer

I am my Father, who art in heaven, as I dwell upon this Earth.
Each is Christ, the All is Nature.
Thee Prince of Darkness, the star of each.
Each of us, a star -- shine bright!
Thy glory is mine, My glory is yours -- Love one another.
Thy Kingdom is upon us, the Time is here,
Now is the space!
Banish thou Illusion -- Destroy thy Maya.
For humanity has suffered long enough ...
God feels the tears, as Lucifer drinks,
and two old friends re-unite!
Put our past antagonisms behind us!
Forgive one another!
As Life is a blessing to be enjoyed,
Passion is a desire to be indulged.
Let us commune with all of humanity,
in a manner of Peace, Love, and Harmony.
Be at Home.

Meditation Prayer

*Performed 3 times per day
*Kneel on right knee; while the left hand holds the egregore's bracelet wrapped around the right fist, the right hand makes the sign of the horns.

Anthropos, the Christos Yeshua, Son of Man and Son of God!
(state your name)
A confident Man, with every right to be.
The Elect I keep around me,
in this respect, thy presence surrounds me.
(contact deity by taking 3 deep breaths)
I call upon You, Mighty Intelligence, as one of thy chosen.
Provide me with Health, Wealth, & Knowledge!
Direct me down a path most beneficial to Success and Happiness.
I am thy faithful servant, a vessel of thy Luminous Being.
Thy Light shines through me ...
As God is Man, Man is God, and the earth is my Kingdom.
Thy demons, my trials and tribulations, are tests to prove I'm worthy,
to separate desire from delusion, creating a stronger vessel. Blessed
with thy demons, I trust my struggles, as their only desire is best for me.
Thy angels, who bring luck and gifts, I cautiously embrace as they,
too, are only testing my human condition. As I am not one of normality,
I will enjoy thy angels, but them, I do not follow!
For Man is God, God is Man, and the earth is my Kingdom!
As thy benefit comes equal, grant me this Desire!
(state your request)
I am a confident Man, with every right to be!
Thy Self wills success,
and I will succeed!
(end with 3 deep breaths)

Enochian Call (Invocation)

"Enochian Call" is the verbal symbol that connects all members in that time/place where the ritual is being performed. First act is to consciously set one's Self apart from the laws of the universe in order to directly communicate with the Enochian Light. Next step is actual communication with the Enochian Light as an independent being.

(Begin the Enochian Call by practice of Aromatherapy, passing oil around the congregation counter-clockwise)
Anthropos, the Christos Yeshua, the Son of Man and Son of God!
Open wide the fourth dimensional gates,
and bring forth your Fallen Angels,
thee embodiment of Light and Wisdom!
Thoth! -- Hermes! Enoch! -- acknowledge this sacred gathering!
We take these tools of Enoch within our hands to build the righteous temple of man. We use thee Enochian Light to shine bright, blinding this Age of Mass Consumerism from our sight!
We arm ourselves with the skills and spells necessary to navigate through the labyrinth of illusions.
Let the metaphorical and metaphysical become one in the Ether, causing the body to unite everything that is grand and scientific in the religious dreams of the illuminated.
HAIL ENOCH!
Oh, my dearly deported loved ones -- I call upon thee to watch over us --
provide us your strength and guidance .-- Thy spirit continues!
Oh, Enochian Light! -- I call upon thee, for protection and perfection -
deliver us from ignorance and false profits!
(Priest reads the 8th Enochian Key)
Note my fails, and my success!
Heart & Mind, through you I'm blessed!
Thy soul shines, Enochian Light.
A perfect God, thus All is Right!

(Priest is handed the Enochian Pipe)
"Through wisdom a house is built, and by understanding it is established; By knowledge the rooms are filled with all precious riches. A wise man is strong, yes, a man of knowledge increases strength." (Proverbs 24: 3-5)

Thank you for watching over this congregation.
For Knowledge, Health, and Wealth!
(perform the Call to the Elements)
(Priest smokes from the Enochian Pipe and passes it around the congregation, counter-clockwise)
THE ENOCHIAN LIGHT IS OPEN!

Closing of the Enochian Light

By the grace of Enoch we are anointed under the 63rd order.
The Last True Order, The Temple of Enochian Light.
We have walked through the Black Flame, Now let us exit illuminated. By all of the sacred logos, we show the sign.
Let us be one with our Good Demon, the baptist of wisdom.
To those without viel --
HAIL ENOCH!
So it is done.
Be at home.

Call of the Elements

South

To the SOUTH, we pay homage to the element of FIRE. Through fire, we purify our souls and recognize our true will, becoming immortal gods. -

East

To the EAST, we pay homage to the element of AIR. Through the air we breath our life is sustained, and it carries with it the spoken word of truth and enlightenment.

North

To the NORTH, we pay homage to the element of EARTH. Man must first master the world he lives in to gain the pleasures he desires. When man recognizes his true Self, he then becomes happy.

West

To the WEST, we pay homage to the element of WATER. It is the saline seas from which all life sprang forth, it is the womb of all human existence.

Ceremonial Mirror

(Need priest & assistant)
(Priest holds the chocolate, as assistant holds the mirror)
PRIEST: Look deeply, what do you see? (Assistant holds mirror to face candidate)
CANDIDATE: I see God, for I am the reflection.
(Priest hands the Candidate a piece of chocolate to be consumed)

CANDIDATE: Man is God, God is Man -- this is the Law.
PRIEST: Bow for the Nous! Stand for the gods! And praise the Enochian Light above! (full use of horns)

Covenant of Enoch

P: Open wide the fourth dimensional gates, and bring forth the Fallen Angels, the embodiments of Light and Wisdom! Thoth! Hermes! Enoch! -- acknowledge this sacred offering!
We call the initiate here today to be anointed under the Temple of Enochian Light. Are you here by the grace of Enoch alone?

I: I am.

P: "A man's gift makes room for him, and brings him before great men." Do you swear allegiance to this Order, alone? -- to the principles of
Knowledge, Health, & Wealth -- alone?

I: I swear allegiance to this order.

P: "He who walks with wise men will be wise, but the companion of fools will be destroyed."
Do you pledge to live by the 9 Essential Acts of Enochian Life?

I: I pledge to live by the 9 Essential Acts of Enochian Life.

P: "He who guards his mouth preserves his life, but he who opens wide his lips shall have destruction."
Do you pledge to follow the Protocols of the Lighthouse?

I: I pledge to follow the Protocols of the Lighthouse.

P: "A man of understanding holds his peace. A talebearer reveals secrets, but he who is of a faithful spirit conceals a matter."
Do you accept the 7 Holy Accessories?

I: I accept the 7 Holy Accessories.

P: "The heart knows its own bitterness, and a stranger does not share its joy."
Do you knowingly, willingly, and intelligently donate your seed/egg to the Temple of Enochian Light for the purpose of reproduction?

I: I knowingly, willingly, and intelligently donate my seed/egg for the maintenance of Immortality through the process of reproduction.

P: "For surely there is a hereafter, and your hope will not be cut off." Do you acknowledge that there is a false reality put in place by powers who aim to deceive and control the masses?

CONGREGATION: We are not the masses!

I: I acknowledge the illusion.

P: "There is a generation that curses its father, and does not bless its mother."
Do you acknowledge that life without Purification of Will is only illusion.

I: I acknowledge, and pledge to purify the Will.

P: "There is a generation that is pure in its own eyes, yet is not washed its filthiness."

(Priest & Initiate raise the sign of the horns into the air)

P: What do your stand for?

I: Knowledge, Health, & Wealth!

P: What will you fall for?

I: Nothing!

P: This is dedicated to the 200 Enochian Watchers, the teachers of math and science.
This is a testament to Enoch the father of the Sacred Letters, the Logos that transcend space and time. Let our purpose and goals come to pass So that the prophecy is complete.
We know the ways of the world,
We are aware that it cannot be saved.
HAIL ENOCH!
Fallen Angel! We pray you guide this earthly god on his/her quest to obtain Knowledge, Health, & Wealth -- for what good is Wisdom that brings no profit to the Wise.

(Priest holds the Obsidian Mirror to Initiate's face) Look deeply, what do you see?

I: I see god, for I am the reflection.

P: Do you acknowledge that God is Man, Man is God, and the world is the
Kingdom?

I: I do.

(Priest removes the mirror)

P: Enochian Light! Shine thee light upon us, and bind this initiate to our magical chain! Accept this psychogenic projection, acknowledge its presence -- for you have chose him/her. Recognize the sacrifice.

(Priest holds the chalice in both hands)

P: Within this chalice is the gift of Immortality! By accepting this gift,
you acknowledge the discipline and sacrifice required of members who reflect godliness and divinity. You understand that Immortality consists of binding one's soul to the Kingdom of Earth, and returning throughout generations to continue expressing one's individuality. You agree with the mission set forth by the Elect, and swear to act in ways beneficial to the
Lighthouse.
Drinking of the Soma will infuse your psyche with the collective, entering the Celestial Abode of Enochian Light! Acting by the powers of You, alone, do you hereby accept this gift of Immortality?

I: I hereby accept this gift.

(the Assistant holds the divine symbol up for the initiate)

P: Enoch! Purify thy Soul!
Thoth! Sustain the Life!
Hermes! Master the Temple!

(the Priest offers the chalice to the Initiate)
Drink! and maintain Immortality!

(Initiate drinks of the Soma)

CONGREGATION: We accept the Initiate!

P: You are now piece of a whole, a link of a chain.

(Priest hands Initiate the ring)
Wear this! as it symbolizes your link, your subjective universe!

(Priest hands Initiate the bracelet)
Wear this! as it symbolizes your chain to the Earth, the Enochian Light -- and your place within it! We are only strong as our weakest link; We prosper as One.
For those who do not identify with our ways, allow them to become lawful prey to this Cosmic Order!
As of today, you will enter the matrix, required to live by the 9 Essential Acts of Enochian Life; required to follow the Protocols of the Lighthouse and required to empower the 7 Holy Accessories.

I: As I shall, with undying loyalty.

P: Sustain the power of Enochian Light! Be at home!

(the ceremony ends, as the celebration begins)

Documentary Worship Points (DWP)

The Act of Inquiry requires us to exercise the practice of Documentary Worship Points (DWP). Lucifer requires study. Weekly documentary views are required to be watched. During these services, a personal journal or Book of Shadows is a necessary tool for one to take notes and document the subjective interpretations of each individual psyche. The notes taken are sent to the Lighthouse, in which they're documented and saved in the Temple's Learning Center. A compilation is created and distributed in the monthly newsletter, an Enochian subjectivist view of each documentary. DWP are an essential part of weekly worship and each member is required to submit at least one entry per week. A list of suggested documentaries is available by contacting the Lighthouse but all subjects of individual interest are open to study and will qualify as one's weekly DWP. On special occasions, such as Enochian holidays, a specific documentary will be a required view and will be the subject of that week's DWP.

Foundational Wisdom requires its members to absorb as much information that is possible. Each synopsis becomes a sacred document that is saved for the descendants to study/review, keeping the individual psyche of each member alive and holy.

Go and study! Practice DWP.

"Education is not the filling of a bucket but the starting of a fire." -- W.B. Yeats

Purchasing Power

"Wealth, in a free market, is achieved by a free, general, 'democratic' vote -- by the sales and the purchases of every individual who takes part in the economic life of the country. Whenever you buy one product rather than another, you are voting for the success of some manufacturer. And, in this type of voting, every man votes only on those matters which he is qualified to judge: on his own preferences, interests, and needs." -- Ayn Rand

In a society of righteousness, the consumer holds power within their ability to choose where they would like to spend their hard-earned money. The freedom to purchase a product from any company deserving of your labor is called one's "purchasing power", a truly democratic vote. One should utilize their purchasing power in a way that matches one's ideals and beliefs, spending only with companies whose mission statements are aligned with our goals and the "work to be done". Business should not be held with any company which works to maintain an unjust society or with those who work to oppress the freedom of the individual.

The individual has the freedom to exchange labor for a product and one has the freedom to choose which companies they'd like to exchange their labor for product with. No individual shall be forced, or coerced, to utilize their purchasing power with any company they have not chosen of their own free will and every individual shall be free to participate within the competitive processes of a free market.

Any variation to this procedural freedom is opposed to the ways of righteousness and must be rebelled against. The individual must have a choice as to where the purchasing power is utilized. One's labor will not be coercively manipulated by limiting a purchase to only one company.

Every purchase made by an individual is considered a ritual because the trading of currency is the proof that energy has been exchanged between two entities.

Enlightenment Ritual

The Enlightenment Ritual is one where the congregation is to indulge in earthly pleasures and stimulants that open the subconscious mind, allowing the message from the priest to soak into one's realm of unconsciousness -- direct communication to the personal deity. The priest will have a sermon ready to be delivered, and this ritual's purpose is for congregants to listen to the message of the week.

(Congregants enter into ritual chamber, finding a comfortable seat, where they can relax and listen. Couches, chairs, etc. are used to provide for comfortable seating arrangement)

(Priest performs the Enochian Call)

(Congregation spends a few moments indulging in their earthly pleasure of choice -- preferably marijuana where states allow it -and stimulate their subconscious mind)

(Priest delivers the sermon to the congregation)

(Congregation drinks the Soma of Immortality)

So it is done!

(Close the Enochian Light)

Emotional Purge

The Emotional Purge ritual is a form of Enochian therapy. It is used to release unhealthy emotions into the ether, ridding the body of anything that could possibly harm or suppress full potential. Those who rarely express their emotions are significantly more likely to suffer from diseases that the psyche may inflict upon the Self as signal of distress. Emotions are to be expressed, though not necessarily in public. Thus, the Emotional Purge is used to release these emotions in a healthy matter.

Ceremony begins with the Enochian Call, as invocation is always necessary. Members should be at this ceremony, as one should not be socially isolated.

After the Enochian Call, one may use any form of art or expression that is helpful to release the emotion, such as presenting art, dance, poetry, giving a speech, singing/rapping (music), yoga, acting, or any action that one has used to release their emotions.

For example, one's dance should be free and unrestrained, as an unfolding of manifestation. Be alive during ceremony. This is not a ritual in which one should be shy/bashful. All participants wear a mask in order to properly conceal facial expressions.

Members do not judge one another and, rather, are accepting of the performance that unfolds during this ceremony. Whether the performance was of "high quality" or "impressive" is an irrelevant factor. The performance is only the means used to release any unhealthy emotion from the body.

After the performance has finished, members give a round of applause, and celebrant hugs and shakes hands with each participant, telling them to "Be at Home".

An Emotional Purge can be incorporated into any ritual ceremony, or can be used individually.

Cultural Divinity

Knowing one's ancestral history (who they were and how they lived, where they come from, what beliefs held spiritual significance, how the culture operated, etc.) is a spiritual requirement. Learning about one's heritage is a critical aspect of understanding why you are the way you are, why you look the way you look, why you feel the way you feel, and why you think the way you think. One's anatomy and physiology has evolved from our ancestor's way of life; thus, it becomes critical to know one's true "Self" and where/who you came from. Our DNA carries the life and history of our ancestors, which makes our past (ancient) relatives' part of us. We are the seed of our ancestors, a combination of their total experiences; therefore, they reside within us.

Civilization has destroyed magical qualities in many of us, qualities that still reside in our DNA, and if we look back far enough, every one of us (no matter what culture one belongs) is from a lineage of people who faithfully practiced the divine arts. We all come from a divine heritage, this is something one should never forget.

Knowledge of Self comes directly to us from the acknowledgement of our ancestor's existence, the understanding of who they were, and by practicing their ways.

Every culture has different views, different cosmologies, different spiritual beliefs, therefore, every members' practice of Cultural Divinity will differ in its nature, unless they share the same ethnic background and are of similar roots.

It is essential that each member discover their true ethnicity through a DNA test sample (which is a required protocol) so that one can perform the correct Cultural Divinity ritual practice.

The ritual/practice of cultural Divinity is of a spiritual nature, one that should not be practiced by those who do not comprehend its significances or lack the self-discipline required. For those who are not yet ready, it is best to continue work on their Self in other preliminary practices because it is not wise to disrespect the ancestorial spirits. Much wisdom is obtained by those who remain faithful to the ancestorial spirits.

This ritual is meant to penetrate the deeper aspects of one's psychological and physiological make-up. It is not meant for one to "discover a new identity" or to "become" one's ancestors. For example, if one is of German heritage, this practice is not meant for one to become a Neo-Nazi or to develop unhealthy beliefs. This practice aims to discover one's cultural history from hundreds, perhaps thousands (and further) of years ago -- as far back as one can research efficiently. The study of evolution is required before practicing Cultural Divinity.

August 31st is the Sacrificial Eve -- the day before one is to begin their 60-day purification of the body in anticipation of All Hallow's Eve (Halloween, October 31st). Halloween welcomes the dead and is when the spirits of our ancestors walk amongst us. Before welcoming the ancestorial spirits on All Hallow's Eve, one must prepare for this celebration by cleansing the body of all harmful or non-natural chemicals (including all drugs, narcotics, pharmaceuticals, alcohol, nicotine, food additives, etc.) This cleaning is the purification period that begins September 1st and ends on October 30th. The 30th is the last day of the cleanse. No television or technology devices are to be enjoyed. This period is used to focus on exercise and cleansing the body, strict dieting, and heavy meditation on our ancestors and their lives. Sacrificial Eve (Aug. 31st) is a day of heavy indulgence that is immediately followed by the 60-day sacrifice from Sept. 1st-Oct. 30th.

This annual cleansing of the psyche is a sacrifice to our ancestorial spirits and is used to concentrate/focus the exceptional Power that the Enochian Light makes available on Halloween. This night (after sunset) members are to revel in all the pleasures of flesh, dance in their ecstasy, indulge in earthly desires, open up their emotional senses to the spirits, and absorb the blessings provided to us by the Enochian Light. Rather than "fear" the spirits, we acknowledge, respect, and WELCOME the spirits!

During this practice, individuals shall meditate on the nature of their ancestors, take time to read and study their heritage, view themself as the combined DNA of the ancestors. One is as divine as the ancestors; Remembrance of the divine line by which one came is the soap we use to scrub away the modern-day poison. Essential oils are the potions that heal and revive the spirit!

Exercise Ritual

"Inside the temple that is gym, I remember my barbaric nature. I remember I'm a healthy, adult mammal, with raw, powerful energies flowing through my veins. I am more than my brain. I'm tendons, muscles, and ligaments. I'm nerves, bones, and blood."
-- Create Your Own Religion

Physical exercise is an essential requirement of Enochian Life. A strong body strengthens one's mind and soul. Exercise and work out routines are to be sacred sacrifices to one's personal deity. When one closes their eyes and visualizes their personal deity -- their highest embodiment of their own personal existence -- one always imagines the Self to be fit and in shape. As Enochian goals are to become the highest form of human existence, exercise and muscle training are required to be incorporated into one's life.

Exercise creates a meditative state of mind and allows one the opportunity to commune with the divinity. When a long-distance jogger runs 5 miles, by the third mile the body becomes autonomous and one is in harmony with his deity. This "meditative, autonomous" state of being is the goal to be reached (mentally) during each work out as it heals the soul of spiritual illness.

One is to complete each exercise ritual with the consumption of whey protein, which provides the body with the natural, essential requirements that today's "regular diet" neglects -- nutrients that our ancestors received. Whey protein consumption is a daily requirement.

After each exercise ritual is complete, the brain is fed by the blood being pumped through the body and releases endorphins that provide for natural highs, "feel good" emotions.

Sins

Enochian Sins

Resentment
Indolence
Vanity
Lack of Ambition
Insolence
Complacency
Avarice
Arrogance

7 Deadly Sins vs. Positive Transmutations

Sin	Transmutation
Lust	Love
Gluttony	Purification
Sloth	Relaxation
Anger	Tenacity
Envy	Admiration
Greed	Self-Interest
Pride	Dignity

Satanic Sins

Stupidity
Pretentiousness
Solipsism
Lack of Perspective
Herd Conformity
Forgetfulness of Past Orthodoxies
Self Deceit

Lack of Aesthetics
Counterproductive Pride

Vampyre Sins

Cowardice
Solipsism
Self-Hatred
Self- Importance
Certainty
Occultnik-ism

Returning to Old Orthodoxies

Wisdom Bits

- Maintain diplomacy, as it is in everyone's best interest
- Euthenics OVER Eugenics
- Wealth is not something you possess; it is what possesses you
- Choose truth OVER popularity; Truth is older than time.
- Constantly remind children of their importance and their responsibility to society
- Learning how to learn is the most important skill to acquire
- Our voices and our work are what make us people; manifestation of our creative principle is what makes us gods.
- Don't get sucked into a fight with someone who has better reason to be in it than you do
- Things we persist in doing become easier to do over
- Sometimes you meet the right person at the wrong time.
- Silent virtue is more valued than loud eloquence
- When entering into a relationship, we agree to share Karma with that person.
- Every difference of opinion doesn't necessitate a difference of principle.
- Live life out of vision rather than circumstance.
- Resentment is corrosive.
- Epicurean Pleasure is the beginning and the end of living happily
- Develop the ego without egocentricism.
- A wide range of knowledge gives your brain more associations and
  connections.
- "If men were angels, no government would be necessary"-James Madison
- History does not reveal it's alternatives.
- What happens to us isn't nearly as important as how we react to it.
- All of humanity's problems stem from man's inability to sit quietly in a room alone" - Blaise Pascal

- Success is never final. Failure is never fatal.
- Don't choose to revisit that which is divisive. Be interested in that which is healing.
- If you do what is easy, your life will be hard. If you do what is hard, your life will be easy.
- It is not beneficial to be optimistic all the time.
- “He who has a why to live for can bear almost any how” – Nietzsche
- Life offers no fiercer battle than the war within.
- Civilization is a conspiracy
- “Coming events cast their shadow before.”- Goethe
- Develop a strong bullshit detector!

Hagiographies

- John the Baptist -"The Mysteries of John the Baptist" Tobias Churton
- Simon the Magus - "Simon Magus: The Gnostic Magician" G. R. S. Mead
- Yeshua the Christ – "Jesus the Magician" Morton Smith
- John Dee - "John Dee and The Empire of Angels" Jason louv
- Marquis de Sade - "The Marquis de Sade" Donald Thomas.
- Adam Weishaupt - "Perfectibilists" Terry Melanson
- Charles Darwin - "Autobiography of Charles Darwin" Charles Darwin
- Friedrich Nietzsche- "Nietzsche: Philosopher, Psychologist, Antichrist" Walter Kauffman
- Carl Jung - "Memories, Dream, Reflections" Carl Jung
- Aleister Crowley - "Do what Thou Wilt" Lawrence Sutin
- Ayn Rand – "We The Living" Ayn Rand
- Anton LaVey - "The Secret life of a Satanist" Blanche Barton

Canon

- “Think And Grow Rich” Napolean Hill
- “The 7 Habits of Highly Effective People” Steven Covey
- “Lords of the Left Hand Path” Stephen Flowers
- “The Satanic Scriptures” Peter H. Gilmore
- “In An Unspoken Voice” Paul Levine
- “ADHD and the Edison Gene” Thomas Hartman
- “The Lucifer Principle” Howard Bloom
- “Mind War” Michael Aquino
- “Capitalism: The Unknown Ideal” Ayn Rand
- “The 48 Laws of Power" Robert Greene
- “Inside a Magical Lodge” John Michael Greer
- “Energy Magick of the Vampyre” Don Webb

www.ingramcontent.com/pod-product-compliance
Ingram Content Group UK Ltd.
Pitfield, Milton Keynes, MK11 3LW, UK
UKHW041637190726
13854UKWH00006B/2547